Yakov Grinshpun was born in the Soviet Union, in a Nazi-controlled Jewish ghetto, at the end of World War II. Brainwashed during the last years of Stalin's rule, he dedicated his life to the regime. The realities of Soviet life gradually led him to disappointment, disillusionment, and distrust. He got tired of his double life—praising the regime as a teacher while hating the system. Rampant anti-Semitism and worsening living conditions led to the desire for change. When the door to Jewish emigration was open by the pressure from the West, he made a difficult and dangerous decision to leave the country for good. After a first unsuccessful attempt, he emigrated at the age of 45. His adjustment in a country with different culture, mentality, and language was difficult and humiliating. However, Yakov didn't just rebuild his old life; he created a new life for himself and his family in the new country.

For Mila: wife, mother, grandmother.

You are greatly missed.

And for our daughter, Rika, and

grandchildren, Sabina and Michael

Yakov Grinshpun

A MAN OF TWO SUPERPOWERS

From Russia with Hope

To Mary, a neighbor who became a friend
Y. Grinshpun

Illustrated by
Inessa Rosenfeld

AUSTIN MACAULEY PUBLISHERS™

LONDON • CAMBRIDGE • NEW YORK • SHARJAH

A CIP catalogue record for this title is available from the British Library.

ISBN 9781398446977 (Paperback)
ISBN 9781398446984 (ePub e-book)

www.austinmacauley.com

First Published 2022
Austin Macauley Publishers Ltd®
1 Canada Square
Canary Wharf
London
E14 5AA

Many thanks to people who made this book possible:

Caren Niele for setting me off on this journey when the English language was a mystery to me.

To Olga Botcharova and Laura Zam for advice and encouragement.

To Inkwell and West Boynton writers' groups.

Table of Contents

Prologue
From Russia with Hope

Then there was the weather. It was—on July 6, 1989, my last day in the USSR—like the country itself, unstable. One moment, the ruby-red stars on the tall Kremlin towers, which had replaced the huge tsarist two-headed copper eagles, just about managed to uphold the ominous skies. The next moment, sunlight set the stars on fire. And then, the rain would start all over again. I saw these changes as we ran to the mall near Red Square for the last-minute purchases. The weather matched my feelings.

We were still packing well into the afternoon. A feeling began in my stomach around three o'clock and started to spread up into my chest, which started to burn. Rubbing my eyes, I noticed tears and was more resigned than surprised. A thought ran through my mind: Severing ties is like separating conjoined twins. Russia was the country of my birth despite the hated regime. Russian was the only language I knew, and the culture saturated my soul. Saying good-bye to everything I knew broke my heart. It was not just the move to another country—it was the move to another culture, another language, and another system. The move was a dream; at the same time, it was a gamble, with all that a gamble entails. Radical uncertainty, with the possibility of a big win—or an equally big loss.

I didn't know what lay ahead, but at least I was getting out. I knew only that getting further from one place was also to come closer to another. I hoped it will be America.

Before leaving for the airport, we were invited for dinner at my uncle's three-room apartment—a luxury by Soviet standards. In the middle of the large rectangular living room stood a few tables pushed together. Overflowing with cheese, kielbasa, cold cuts, herring, home-made food, and vodka, they represented an island of stability.

After a hectic day, it was a relief to sit down for an early dinner. I took my place of honour at the head of the table. My wife Mila sat to my right. She was in her early forties, as beautiful as she had been when I first saw her in a remote village about two decades earlier. Her large, dark eyes radiated warmth, despite what we had gone through the past year. To my left sat my brilliant daughter Rika, excited and tentative, who had just graduated university with a degree in mathematics. The surrounding members of our extended family talked little, apparently preferring to keep their feelings to themselves.

"This is the Last Supper," I said, with a half-smile.

"And you are the Judas at this table, the betrayer of the Fatherland." My cousin Boris never missed an opportunity to be witty.

My mother-in-law shook her head but didn't say a word. She didn't have to. A few people laughed, I didn't.

"Thank you for coming…" I lost the trail of my thoughts.

The joke didn't lighten the mood, and the conversation hit an uncomfortable lull. Silence enveloped the table. *It's no joke to take the risk of packing up and moving to an unfamiliar world. As the first in the family to leave, I show the way.*

"It's raining. How long will it take to get to the airport?" my father-in-law Leonid asked, breaking the silence. Most of us gazed out the window. Droplets of rain ran down the glass like tears. *Does the country cry for us?*

My mother-in-law Fanya wrinkled her brow. "Maybe we should leave earlier than planned?"

Now everyone was staring through the windows, faces as gloomy as the sky. The farewell party had come to resemble a funeral. The sun was, I could sense, in a deadlock with the grey sky, as shafts of light penetrated the clouds. With all my heart, I wanted the sky to clear.

"Look how much vodka we have!" My brother-in-law Val raised the nearest bottle. "Do they have gefilte fish or vinaigrette like this in America? Eat it while you can, and let's have a drink!"

The conversation picked up after that. I looked down at the mosaic of golden gefilte fish, reddish vinaigrette, greenish *kholodets* (a jellied meat dish), white bread, brown bread, and, of course, crystal clear cold vodka, the companion of *kholodets*. We all filled our plates, but no one would think of starting before the first toast. *When will I see it all again?* Vodka to bitter thoughts is like water to fire. It is the remedy for a lot of things.

I proposed a toast. "Let's drink—"

"You can end right there." That was Boris, he could never stop joking.

With a Russian winter-cold glance in his direction, I continued, "Let's toast that we meet soon, rather in America."

We drank the Russian way, of throwing back vodka and right away chasing the vodka with an assortment of *zakuska* to kill the aftertaste. *Zakuska* may be the one Russian idiom for which there is no adequate translation. It is a general term for anything that can be eaten as an accompaniment to vodka. There can be no *zakuska* without vodka; otherwise, it's just plain food.

Quiet ensued, and minutes passed while we blunted our hunger. As I chewed and swallowed, I continued to watch through the windows at the gathering clouds. Little by little a few comments were exchanged, but I didn't listen. *What awaits us at Customs?* A sudden silence brought me back to the table. I had failed to notice a question.

"I will miss this," I said, to no one in particular.

After a couple of toasts, everyone's mood improved, smiles reappeared, and the black clouds, as if answering my prayers, whirled away, leaving in their wake a blue sky.

"Don't worry; we will send you the leftover *zakuska*," said my aunt, the hostess.

Glasses were refilled, the conversation picked up, and the laughter bubbled. It seemed for a while as though everybody had forgotten the bittersweet occasion that had brought us together. But after the next toast, the conversation changed direction once more.

"This is your last day in the country," someone said, "so let's drink to seeing you again."

At this stage of the dinner, it didn't matter that the toasts repeated themselves. I set down my knife and fork a little harder than I'd intended. Picking up my glass, I said, "I have a counter toast. Let's drink to me being a rich man to be able to visit you. It's our last day as citizens—oh, sorry. I forgot that they already took away our citizenship. It's our last day as residents of this country, but let's hope one day we'll be back. Not permanently, of course."

People were running out of toasts. The dinner had reached a plateau. One person burped, another leaned back in his chair rubbing his stomach, and a few went out to the balcony for a smoke. My aunt and mother-in-law collected empty dishes and disappeared into the kitchen. The rest of us stayed silent until the women returned with the main course: Kiev cutlets and buckwheat kasha with *varnechkes*. Boris flapped his hands towards his nose and near inhaled them. Sleepy people awoke, relaxed ones straightened up like soldiers called to attention, and smokers hurried to their seats. We filled our plates with the new food so fast that one would never have known we had just taken in a lot of *zakuska*. Glasses clinked; knives hit plates. Hot butter burst from the interiors of the golden cutlets. Each forkful of the cutlets I savoured as if it were something I would never be able to taste again.

One more quick toast, then silence fell over the room again. When the cutlets were gone, a few more toasts followed. Only one of them—for the hands that had made this divine dish—made any sense. *Is this the only way we can communicate, through toasts?*

Then my niece Ada, daughter of my half-sister Riva and only two years younger than I, out of the blue asked, "Why did you decide to leave the country?"

The mood changed—yet again. I opened my mouth and shut it, tried again, but no words emerged. I couldn't find the answer to her simple question. As all eyes converged on me, there was quite a long period of silence.

"Come on," Mila said.

It took another shot for me to come up with a boring answer, "I wanted a different life for our daughter." I took a breath and continued, "And maybe for all of us."

Not only was it boring, but it also was not the real answer.

My niece, a smart cookie, didn't seem convinced.

"You know," she said, "when you decided last year to leave, I couldn't stop thinking about what we should do. I felt we should leave, too. I hoped your answer will help convince my husband."

"It's raining again." My father-in-law looked at his watch. "We'll have to leave earlier than we'd planned."

We drank the last toast, and everybody wished us a safe trip. The farewell ceremony started. We hugged, kissed, and thanked everyone for coming to see us off.

"And now let's sit down," my mother-in-law commanded.

We all sat for a silent moment before the journey, a Russian custom. Not that it would make the trip less difficult or stressful.

The question my niece had asked stuck with me on the way to the airport. Lost in thoughts, I tried to put together the rationale for our leaving. As the end of my Soviet life approached, my mind circled back to the beginning, both of my life and the decision-making process. I thought back to the time when the idea to leave took root, and I tried to recreate my path. It did not happen when I was young. At one point, we were young, happy, and, paradoxically, free. We lived, we loved, and we laughed, despite everything. In the West, everyone assumes Communism was a great evil. Various aspects were evil—a lot of them. But it wasn't all grey and dreary. We were humans just like everyone else. We had our dreams, our crushes, our loves, and our petty animosities.

There's an old joke.

"Grandpa," a boy asked, "When was it better, under Stalin, Khrushchev, Brezhnev or Gorbachev?"

"Of course, under Stalin!"

"Why?"

"All the girls were young and beautiful then."

Things changed as we grew up and realised that there was little happiness without dignity; only crushed dreams without freedom.

Once I began exhuming the past, my memory woke and napped at will, bringing back blurry views, muted sounds, and dissipated smells. The memory dulled or sharpened events bringing me again into abandoned spaces and times. The shoots of it twisted, curled, and tightened around all I knew. When all is said and done, the only real thing I took with me, besides my family, were my memories. My memories were who I was.

I was suspicious of them—they could be irrelevant, as well as inaccurate. Moreover, they are erratic; the past dates change, places mix up, and chronologies adjust. When called upon, memories slip away and return at the time that suits them. Stories mix and mingle; facts grow new shoots. Memories are stored in a mixed-up manner, not chronologically, not alphabetically, not even according to significance. They are faulty because they insist on filling in the blanks. Memories hardly arrange themselves into chapters. Not mine, anyway. Decades might be a better form of organization for me. My transformation that led to the decision to leave the USSR more or less fits into three consequent decades. Each made me aware of one of the three reasons that led to the desperate choice to get out. Trying to pinpoint the time and single out the one element of the long decision-making process is like trying to take hold of a wave in a swelling sea. Because I drew from my own unique memories, my story may be different from how others saw the events. As a Hasidic proverb says, "What is truer than truth? It is the story."

Events run hot and cold in my head. But the dark recollections explained the reasons for my exodus. So, although my memories refused to line up chronologically, there was a thread that connected most of them. They evoke in me similar emotional responses: fear, disgust, and shame. Step by step, I have assembled the fragments of my past in an incomplete picture of what forced me to leave my country of birth. Interwoven with happy memories, a sad picture of what led me to the choice emerged.

So, the question remained: Why the decision to leave the land where I was born, the land I brought my daughter into, the land of generations of my ancestors? How and when did it all begin? What was the pivotal point? As my life in the Soviet Union was coming to an end, it seemed to me that most of the events that led to that decision fell into three categories. The three reasons for my leaving the Soviet Union were anti-Semitism, corrupt politics, and dire economics. My disbelief, disillusionment, and disappointment each fuelled my burning desire to get out of what I came to see as a hell on earth. These reasons planted seeds that grew, blossomed, and bore fruit. Each matured at a different pace, came to fruition at a different time, and had a different significance. But they didn't contradict each other. They reinforced each other until the decision stood unyielding on its own, like a three-legged stool.

So, my answer to my niece's question began to take shape on that ride to the airport. The passage of time had allowed me a bird's-eye view of my meandering road to that fateful choice when I realized that real life differed from what they taught and made to believe in and that the best solution was to run away.

So, as we Jews are known to do, I will begin with an attempt to answer my niece's question with a question: What was the difference between the teachings and the reality of Soviet life?

Part I
I Am Different

Chapter 1

I started as an innocent child standing unprepared on the brink of challenges, choices, and opportunities.

Born into a Jewish family, I didn't know what it means to be a Jew. Before school, I didn't know that I am different because of being Jewish. At seven years old, I got my first taste of what it meant.

It was early autumn, a perfect time to explore the courtyard during a big break in the middle of the school day. We played ball and enjoyed ourselves. One boy, upset about me scoring a goal, pushed me. I pushed him back. He pulled himself to his feet and rushed at me. During this fist-fight with my first-grade classmate, in no complicated manner, he taught me a lesson. We exchanged punches and I seemed to be winning the fight. Out of the blue, he shouted, "Zhid." Zhid is a Russian curse word for a Jew—an ugly word with an ugly meaning. Kike sounds mild compared to it. All American curses are milder than the Russian ones. Russian is a rich language for cursing with various filthy possibilities to insult.

My eyes went wide and my hand fell. As a boxer seeing an opening, the boy punched me in the nose, hard. Blood rushed from my nose taking along my innocence. *Wow, I'm a Zhid. What does it mean?* I looked at my friend Leonid whose eyes were wide open. But what forever etched on the wall of my memory is the image of that yard and the boy's face.

Telling my teacher about the incident didn't look like the right thing to do. I decided also not to tell my parents what happened in that schoolyard, but when my mother noticed blood on my shirt, I told her what took place there.

"You are Jewish, and lots of people don't like Jews. Just walk away when you hear the word next time," she said.

"Why," I asked.

"Just walk away. You will understand it later."

"Mama, had something like that happened to you when you went to school?"

"No. I didn't go to school. And now go and do your homework."

My parents grew up before the revolution and their experiences differed from mine. They, like most people in the shtetl, had no more than three or four years of schooling if that. Shtetl is a Yiddish word for a settlement somewhere between a village and a town where most Jews lived before the Bolshevik revolution.

Right there and then, I learned I was different because of being Jewish. After that, I began identifying myself as such. Until that time, I'd lived in beautiful oblivion, safe in my solid and, in ways, beautiful childhood, unaware of the world's realities. My parents had sheltered me from Soviet life. We were not, by any stretch, wealthy but a well-to-do family by Soviet after-war standards. My parents loved and fed me. I grew up in a culture where feeding meant to love and care. I can argue that, as my mother's only and late child, I was spoiled in comparison to my cousins.

As a child, I knew I was Jewish but didn't know what it meant. Certain things, growing up in a shtetl, you just know. It was my life. Older people spoke Yiddish, we ate chicken soup every Friday night, and yes, my parents fasted on Yom Kippur. After decades of living under a dictatorial anti-religious and anti-Semitic regime, many Jews like myself born after the late 1930s had only tenuous and faded ties to Judaism and the Yiddish language. I did not feel Jewish and did not care much that I was. Just traditions kept by the family. I could not change anything about being Jewish. Even if I wanted, I could not. In my country, I didn't have that choice. If my parents were Jewish—on my birth certificate, they were identified as such—I was Jewish. You don't choose to be born Jewish, but, later in life, you must choose whether it matters to you or not. I was glad I was born Jewish, it just happened. Often people say they are proud to be born Jewish. I think it's similar to saying I am proud to be born on Wednesday. I was, though, proud of Jewish history and Jewish contribution to humankind as I learned little by little about it. I never became an ardent Zionist, but I never stopped being a Jew. I was a Jew by blood. Not by blood of my ancestors in my veins, but by the blood that flowed out from their veins for centuries.

To overcome the forced-on-us uncomfortable feeling of being Jewish, I longed for Jews I could be proud of.

"You know, Karl Marx was Jewish," my friend Leonid told me one day.

"No, he was German," I said.

"No. My father said he was Jewish, and he knows everything. You can ask him."

When I did, he confirmed it.

"Do you know other famous Jews," I asked.

"Yes. There are many, Albert Einstein, for instance."

"Yeah, but both are from the past and other countries," I said, pulling my ear and narrowing my eyes. After a moment, "Do you know Jews worthy of admiration here and now?"

"Chess player, world champion Botvinnik is one."

They filled the void for a while and lifted my spirit. My generation experienced its Jewishness by and large not in a religious but in a spiritual way.

Being Jewish, I wanted to learn more about our history and the traditions we were, for better or worse, a part of. It was during the middle of Stalin's anti-Semitic campaigns that I started school, and the world grew all of a sudden bigger, introducing me to a different reality I couldn't yet comprehend. The regime did not give a damn about what I wanted to learn. In school, they taught me what they wanted me to know. What the regime wanted was to grow little communists who didn't ask questions. They promised no less than the creation of a 'new Soviet man' filled with selfless devotion to the common good who was above all the part of a whole, rather than an individual. That's why Soviet leaders had always been mediocre. The ignorant, ill-educated leaders were obsessed with changing the country to their worldview and cultural level.

We also had to learn the Moral Code of the Builder of Communism, the Catechism of Soviet propaganda that affirms the superior morality of Soviet people who unlike people in capitalist countries were equal in every regard. For a while, this was my compass. In the beginning, we spent little time learning to read and count. First, we had to memorized the anthem of the Soviet Union. We learned it before we learned to read. I still remember it. The anthem implied that the many peoples comprising the so-called Soviet people were *brotherly* peoples united by the Russian big brother. In reality, I grew up discovering and feeling that I'm not a brother, but a hated stepchild.

"You are the future of Communism," my first-grade teacher, Serafima Abramovna, lectured us. She was a Jewish woman in her thirties wearing, as a rule, a below-knee skirt and knitted jacket above colourless blouses she changed weekly.

"You are to follow the party leaders, the members of Politburo—the governing body of the Communist Party." She continued after a pause in a solemn voice, "First of all, our *Vozhd*, our Supreme Leader comrade Stalin." She pointed to a picture of Stalin.

In every classroom, there was an image of Stalin. In my classroom, we had a famous picture—the iconic photograph of Grandpa Stalin holding a little girl. No Soviet school could do without this kind of picture, like none of the remaining churches in the country could do without an icon of the Virgin Mary holding baby Jesus. We recognized Stalin from the day we were born because his image was in every government office, including schools and 'birthing houses' as maternity wards were called in Russian. This didn't count all the publications where his portraits were a must.

"And this is," Serafima Abramovna continued after a minute of sombre silence, "a portrait of comrade Beria, a member of Politburo." After a long silence, "He is the head of the NKVD." NKVD was the predecessor of KGB. We were trained to recognize all members of the Politburo. Every classroom had one of their portraits. Every day we were dragged from classroom to classroom until we could tell them apart. It wasn't easy. Their mediocre faces looked the same at first.

After we learned to read, our teacher showed us a picture of Lenin when he was a little boy.

"You should be like him: honest, hardworking, and obedient," Serafima Abramovna said.

She taught us obedience. First, she trained us how to sit: eyes on a blackboard, back stiff, arms folded, right arm over left. To ask a question, we had to raise the right arm right at ninety degrees to the desk still keeping the elbow on it.

"Then"—she put her finger up—"you wait until I call on you to talk."

Talking among ourselves was never permitted in class. Only when she sharply called a question and, next, a name, we should leap up and spit out the answer. To be hard-working like young Lenin, I raised my hand at ninety degrees keeping my elbow on the desk. When the teacher acknowledged me, I raised half of my desktop; the old hinges squeaked and spoke before me. I leaped up, almost collapsed, and said, "I will be the blackboard wiper."

The lesson I received in the schoolyard differed from the lessons they taught inside the school, but listening to preaching adults, I believed every sweet message.

From the first grade, the system raised me to be a patriot, a proponent of Communism, and a worshiper of Lenin and Stalin. Everything was designed to instil an appreciation for Communism and reverence for its leader, the dear comrade Stalin. As a big part of our early education, we had absorbed Soviet propaganda. We repeated the Party slogans like parrots: *Proletarians of all countries, unite! All power to the Soviets! Peace to the Peoples!* I began to be a little communist in the early 1950s, during the last years of Stalin. I was in awe of the system, I believed in it. For me, at that time, the Soviet Union was the best country in the world, a land filled with hope. The win in World War II, first in space, the superpower status made me proud of my country. Over time, a growing scepticism, a slide into cynicism, disillusionment, and alienation contributed to the unravelling of the communist web I believed in. Multiple events during the years were bit by bit, changing my outlook on my country. and created an overwhelming desire to get out despite all the fears, doubts, and repercussions. But this came later.

Chapter 2

In the 1950s, the first three grades were rather innocent. The real assault on our minds and souls started when we joined the Young Pioneers—the Soviet communist organization for children between ten and fourteen. The Party recognised the importance of childhood indoctrination and pursued it with vigour.

Twenty-two years from now, when they realised they made a mistake in not starting the process in earnest from the very beginning, when my daughter, Rika, I didn't yet know I will have, entered school, they started the process in first grade. The well-oiled propaganda machine invented a thing called Little Octobryonok named for October the month of the Bolshevik revolution. Understanding the crucial importance of symbols, they fastened on the first-graders holiday uniform the five-pointed red star pin—the emblem of the Soviet Union—embellished with baby Lenin circled in the centre. On the day Rika was to become a Little Octobryonok, I told her, "It's an important day for you. You won't be a baby anymore." She couldn't wait to leave for school. When she came home with the star pinned to her holiday uniform, I said, "Congratulations, you are a big girl now. I'm so proud of you." I kissed her on both cheeks. "I bought a cake and when mama comes home, we would have a celebration." It didn't matter that I stopped believing in this nonsense. I, remembering my experience when my parents were not enthusiastic when I became a Pioneer and my vow not to do the same to my children, feigned interest, and she bought it.

Back to early November 1953. In a solemn ceremony on the eve of the 36th anniversary of the Great October Socialist Revolution, my classmates and I had been admitted to the Pioneer Organization. All hypocrisy aside, becoming a pioneer was a significant coming-of-age milestone for a Soviet child. With crisped ironed white shirts and little red kerchiefs like a necktie, we were indoctrinated into the Soviet youth movement.

We stood in a row, all thirty of our third grade. In front of us, along the opposite wall of the corridor, thirty seven-graders with one red kerchief around their necks and another stretched on their palms. We took the oath that we rehearsed many times after school.

"I, Yakov Grinshpun, joining the ranks of All-Union Pioneer Organization, in the presence of my comrades, solemnly promise: to love and protect my Fatherland, to live as the Party teaches us, and to carry out the rules of the Pioneers of the Soviet Union."

The seventh-grader played the horn. He blew so hard that his face turned as red as his pioneer tie. His comrades were putting the ties around our necks. The red around our necks announced to everyone that we were no longer just kids; we were the future builders of Communism. I wore my Young Pioneer tie with pride.

On that cold and cloudless day, I walked home after school in high spirits and full of importance. A road, with rows of nondescript houses marching down the hill towards the small river, led me to my house. The little red tie warmed my chest, and the world was mine to conquer. The sun was distant and cool and the wind icy. Leaves crunched beneath my feet. On the trees, about naked for the winter, I just noticed the frozen frizzy red leaves. I inhaled a lungful of the chilled air. The world smelled fresh as if everything could now start over. I unbuttoned my coat for everyone on the street to see my red tie and pulled up my collar and shoved my hands deep into my pockets. I hoped passers-by would ask me about it. No one did. At home, to my disappointment, there were only lukewarm congratulations. The way we were brought up was not to question adults and to hide our feelings. So, after eating my dinner in silence, I retreated into a corner with a book, pretending to read. Never, I vowed, that would happen to my children when they become pioneers. It would be a memorable day for them.

There was a sense of satisfaction at being a pioneer in the formal procedures and rituals at meetings and parades the school required us to attend. Parades were my favourite. At this time, I didn't see attending parades as a chore and looked forward to the march. On May 1 and November 7, all across the Soviet Union, from Moscow to the edges of the country, from mountains to the northern seas, as the famous song went, people, willingly or unwillingly, celebrated these 'holy' holidays and took part in the spectacles. Showing off had great importance for the regime and attendance was mandatory, weather notwithstanding, from the great Moscow parades to the small towns like mine. The Moscow ones with their rows of tanks and lines of missiles rolling through the Red Square energized, so they say, our patriotism and frightened our enemies. We had the best parades in the world. Macy's parades with their balloons were no comparison to Soviet ones with their missiles.

May 1, the Day of Workers Solidarity, was my favourite parade. In a rural area, for a kid, nothing, even a birthday party, could be more exciting than marching together with all people dressed in their best clothes, to pledge allegiance to the Party and Fatherland. At ten in the morning, the spring sun caressed us like a loving Mother, the deep blue skies opened the whole world, and the huge open-air show of red flags, portraits of leaders, and ridiculous banners generated a big spectacle. Among a sea of white shirts and red ties, I felt like being a part of something big and forgot that several of the kids called me ugly names. We were one—Young Pioneers, the future of Communism. Years would pass until I understood that the actions of children were a symptom, not the problem.

We waited with anticipation for teachers to assign the flags, the banners, and the portraits. The best student received the portrait of our dear Vozhd Stalin. Once, my principal gave it to me. I felt that everybody's eyes were on me. My hands were shaking. It would have been a disaster to drop the image. After that, we walked from the school to the park for the rally. The sky was blue, the day warm, the tall trees and the new grass, green as we were, soft under my feet. As I walked, I saw among the trees, on a wide clearing, on a permanent podium erected for such occasions the local Party leadership like a small version of the Politburo on top of Lenin's mausoleum. They all head caps or fedoras that sheltered their already red faces. They talked to each other, but I couldn't hear them with dozens of people talking around me. The girls were carrying beautiful bouquets of spring flowers, the boys carried banners with catchy slogans, the gymnasts showing off their prowess. The best thing came when a big shot from the podium barked,

"Young Pioneers! To the cause of Lenin, be ready!"

After a three-count delay, we yelled with a sharp salute, *"Always ready!"*

It was the best thing about the parades when I imagined how people looked at me saluting with my arm at the forty-five-degree angle. I remember the park as a place of clear light and sweet air filled with the smell of spring green. Maybe the best thing was our parents giving us a few rubles to enjoy candies and ice cream after the parades. Ice cream, in my shtetl, was available only on special days like these.

November 7 commemorated the Great October Revolution. Once I asked my teacher:

"Why do we celebrate the October revolution in November?"

"Because before 1918, Russia followed the Julian calendar thirteen days behind the Gregorian one used by the rest of the world,"—she explained—"Bolsheviks moved the country into the modern world."

These parades, because of the weather, were less festive. But I still got pleasure from them. While I cared little about the reasons for the celebration, I enjoyed the parades themselves. For me, as for many of us far behind the Iron Curtain, Communism and its rituals—meetings, salutes, slogans, and parades—

in ways replaced religion. Communism, like Christianity, promised a bright future after a difficult past. That is if one believed in either of them. But believing in God seemed stupid to me, a Young Pioneer, who had already known for sure, from the first grade, that God didn't exist. Of course, before the revolution, there was a synagogue, an orthodox church, and a catholic church in my town. In the 1920s Bolsheviks closed them. Since then, the synagogue became grain storage; the orthodox church was blown up and from the remains, they built a high school that I later attended, and the catholic church was half destroyed by a bomb during World War II. This didn't bother me. I agreed with what the Bolsheviks did to these institutions. I have never been to a synagogue in the Soviet Union. My only experience with Judaism was—before I went to school—attending with my father prayers in private houses where older people gathered on High Holidays. With no God, no family history to stick with, and no ability to learn the history on my own, I was a piece of wax in the hands of the Soviet propaganda machine. The school system moulded young communists. Being called a Zhid couldn't undermine my beliefs in Communism yet.

The rituals and the words that accompanied them sounded great for me, until I started, subconsciously at first, to notice contradictions between them and the reality: the treatment of Jews, the long bread lines, and the lack of necessities. I was becoming a little bit disenchanted, not understanding why. That had caused an uncomfortable feeling. But we build defences against unwanted feelings quicker than fleeing from big dogs. As part of our early education, we absorbed the Soviet party line. We were a school of little fishes in the huge sea of propaganda, immersed in songs, meetings, and parades. Our teachers, whether sincerely—and in most cases, they were—or not, took care of our patriotic upbringing. As an ordinary Soviet child, from the first grade forward, they moulded me to be a patriot, a proponent of Communism.

Besides talking about the high ideals of Communism, teachers also talked to us about 'them'. 'They' were the people of the West, above all the American imperialists. Our teachers had nothing good to say about them. By the way, as of the moment of writing, nothing good is said about Russia in the West either. While learning how bad capitalism was, I began to realize that not everything was perfect in the socialist society. Even for a dedicated Young Communist like myself, it became rather difficult to reconcile the promise of a bright future with the realities of life. Still, for me, the Soviet Union was not an 'evil empire', it was home to my only childhood. I still was a little communist ready to die for the cause. Both, the Young Pioneer and later Komsomol (Young Communist League) organizations, as well as our teachers, with their half-truth, hadn't prepared me for real life. My mentality had been shaped by a strong link between the system I lived in and my Jewish identity.

Chapter 3

My parents didn't teach me how to navigate Soviet reality either. By the time I became conscious of these contradictions, people who would dare to question the propaganda were no longer around. My parents didn't engage in the kind of conversations with political undertones that could plant a seed of doubt. They were non-political and for the most part uninvolved in my patriotic upbringing. To my disappointment, they never joined the Party. They were afraid to talk to me not only about political issues but also about Judaism.

One day, my third-grade teacher, Serafima Abramovna—in Russia we had one teacher for the first four grades—talked to us about Pavlik Morozov.

"Pavlik Morozov"—she read from a textbook—"a Young Pioneer, discovered that his father, chairman of the village Soviet council, had conspired with wealthy peasants to hide the grain from state procurement officials. Pavlik informed the authorities. The father and other conspirators were brought to the revolutionary Justice." She paused and scanned the class. "The enemies of the people murdered Pavlik." She stopped reading and didn't speak for a few moments. You could hear a fly in the classroom.

"You have to be like him"—he raised her finger—"or at least try." After a pause, she asked, "Who wants to be like Pavlik?" Thirty hands went into the air, forgetting to keep the elbows on the desk. Next, she said, "Who can tell why you want to be like Pavlik?" Only a few hands went up, including mine. This time we kept the elbows on the desks. The answers were—he was honest, courageous, a good pioneer. When it was my turn, I said, "Because he supported our Party."

"Good answer." The teacher said. I sat smiling.

"At home, you will finish reading the story," she said before dismissing the class.

At home, with a piece of bread with butter in one hand and the book in the other, I began reading. I didn't get up until I finished the story. The USSR glorified Pavlik Morozov as a martyr. The Party used him as a model for young communists for several generations of Soviet schoolchildren. He was adopted by the Young Pioneers as their patron saint. *He is a real hero. I would be honest, courageous, and faithful to the cause of the Party like Pavlik.* We didn't choose our heroes.

At dinner, my father, as a rule, asked me about my day. I was eagerly waiting for the wall clock to show dinner time, mesmerized by the pendulum going from right to left and then from the left to the right, clicking with each turn. At last, we sat for dinner, and my father picked up the fork and asked, "What did you learned and did today?"

"Today my teacher told us about Pavlik Morozov," I smiled. "And at home, I finished reading a story about him. He was a real hero and the enemies of the people murdered him. I want to be like him."

My father put the fork down and looked at me without saying a word. I glanced at my mother and didn't like her facial expression. I switched my eyes back to Father. He still had his fork down.

"So, you want to be like him."

"Yes, I want to be courageous and honest." I put my shoulders back and restrained an urge to salute.

"So, you would do what he did, right?"

"What do you mean?" I said still smiling.

"Would you tell on me?" He still didn't resume eating.

"No… You are not like his father." My small smile disappeared.

"But if I were?" He looked at me and waited.

"I… I… I don't know." My eyes began to well. I looked at my plate and picked up the fork. My eyes were at the plate for the remainder of the dinner. After the dinner of boiled potatoes and schmaltz herring, I retreated to another room and tried to read the story about Pavlik again, but my thoughts were not on reading. *Is my father wrong? Is my teacher right?* Once I went to bed, my eyes welled again. This time I didn't hold tears back.

Only when I matured, I understood my parents' reaction and saw Pavlik Morozov as a tragic symbol of the pressures Stalinism exerted on families. But he remained a hero to me throughout most of my teen years. It was easy to manipulate young brains and fill them with communist propaganda when parents were afraid to say something different. As a child, I heard adult conversations. Often, I didn't understand what they were talking about, and I didn't care. In most cases, conversations fell silent when I entered the room. The conversation about Pavlik Morozov was a rare occasion when my father talked to me about politics—nothing to counterbalance the state's massive propaganda apparatus. Years of programming were not without effect. I was so indoctrinated that one day, after a lecture at school, I came home and told my father I was so proud he is a worker and not a general. I don't remember why a general. I think at the lecture, they compared workers with generals. Without guidance, I unconditionally believed Soviet propaganda: We lived in the best country in the world led by the greatest leader of all times who would bring us into the "communist paradise." We had to be grateful to comrade Stalin for our happy childhood and feel blessed to be born in a magnificent country. We felt bad for those with the misfortune to be born in capitalist countries.

As I meander the maze of my Soviet childhood memories, I find them infused with propaganda.

It's normal to love your childhood, cloudless, and care-free to a certain point. We were not afraid to go to school by ourselves from kindergarten on. We visited our friends without invitation. We safe and sound played in the streets till dusk. I believed my childhood was happy despite not having enough food and toys. We used to make our own toys. I didn't understand the severity of my country's financial and social hardships. Shortages of every kind defined the post-war years in the country. But I didn't know better. Any temporary difficulties, we were told, were the results of World War II and the Western imperialists, who after the war were trying to destroy the first country of workers and peasants. It's interesting, but for a long time, I thought that imperialist and capitalist were synonyms. That communists, who I believed were superior to capitalists, could be imperialists as well didn't occur to me at that time. I prepared myself to defend my country and defeat imperialists in the future war.

Chapter 4

I spent my whole childhood under the shadow of the Great Patriotic War, as they called World War II in the Soviet Union and its grim memories. As a child, I didn't understand the tragedy of the war that took tens of millions of lives to save civilization from collapse and me having a chance at life. A few of the lives lost during the war would bear the names of my relatives. I remember the fun things—running around with friends, unsupervised, playing war. Playing the German invasion was the most popular game among boys. We divided the whole world into 'ours' and Germans who we called Fritzes. Any enemies of Russia during its whole history were Germans or fascists to us. Later, I learned that Russians were better to the Jews than Germans but not by much. That was reflected in an *anekdot*.

There is a Russian, a German, and a Jew. And God says to them, I'll grant you one wish each, any wish you like. Kill all the Germans, yells the Russian. Kill all the Russians, the German screams. And what you want, God asks the Jew. "Grant them both their wishes"—says the Jew—"and I will have a cup of coffee."

I was born under Nazi occupation in a ghetto in the small Jewish shtetl of Chechelnik, in Ukraine. So, I am a Holocaust survivor, sort of, although I lived under Nazis only for about the first two months of my life. When I learned about Nazi atrocities towards Jews, and the Soviet regime didn't talk much about that, I wondered how my family survived at all. My older half-sister, Riva, in her late teens at the start of the war, told me, "We were 'lucky' that the Germans just went through and by the end of the summer of 1941 transferred Chechelnik to the Transnistria area under Romanian control. The Romanians weren't as vicious as Germans." I tilted my head and shrugged.

"The Romanians deported tens of thousands of Jews from Romania and Moldova," she explained. "Hundreds of them ended up in Chechelnik. For our family, it turned out to be good."

I narrowed my eyes, and after a long pause, she continued, "Among the deportees were pharmacists—one of them became my husband—and physicians. And one of the latter was a gynaecologist who saved you and your mother."

"Me?"

"Yes. Because you unsuccessfully tried to drop out into the world legs and ass first. It was the wrong way. He turned you around."

There were not many people in my life who pointed me the right way.

Among the refugees were my mother's oldest sister Shiva with her three children. They came on foot from a nearby shtetl of Kodyma about twenty-five kilometres west. Her husband had died during the trip and they just left him on the roadside. We later found out that all the Jews who remained in Kodyma perished. Three of my mother's other sisters, who lived in Odessa evacuated deep into the Soviet Union where they survived the war. Husbands of two of the sisters died on the battlefield. The husband of the youngest sister, Sonya, survived because he was considered essential for the defence plant and was evacuated east.

After the war, in 1946, all the surviving family members on my mother's side, but one, gathered in Chechelnick when my mother's sisters returned from the east of the country. I was only two and didn't know all the stories about their lives during the war that they shared. I wish I could ask them now.

As I'm writing this, I'm looking at a black-and-white photo no bigger than a postcard taken at the reunion of the surviving members of my mother's family after the war.

In the photograph—frozen in the instant in which it was taken—are my mother, four of her sisters, two of the husbands, and seven children, five of them fatherless. Also, there is my only grandparent who was alive after I was born, but I don't remember him. I am the youngest in the picture. Not in the photo two of my mother's brothers. One of them, Monya, was in love with a gentile girl and didn't want to leave Odessa. He perished during the German occupation. The other brother, Syoma, was in prison and couldn't come. Although the photo was black-and-white, this event was one of the rare bright and joyful moments.

On my father's side of the family, my two cousins were not so lucky. Lisa, the daughter of my aunt Rachel, was taken by the Nazis before I was born. She never came back. Then, I remember in the late fifties they put a list of students from my school who gave their lives protecting the country. One name was Grigoriy Grinshpun.

"He was Uncle Moishe's son," my father said when I asked him.

He was my first cousin, and that was the first time I heard of him. I didn't get a chance to know them. My having learned about them made no difference to them. They were dead. It did make difference to me. The war took them who I might have like.

My half-brother, Mika, from my father's first marriage who was sixteen when the war started, was evacuated by authorities because he was close to the drafting age. In a couple of years by 1943, he was fighting the Nazis. He lost his right leg at the age of nineteen. Without the leg, Mika had a chance on life. The war was a significant part of my family's history, like every family in the country. The war and the Holocaust made my family smaller.

Although the Romanians were not as brutal as Germans, by the end of 1941, the Romanian occupiers created a ghetto that housed about a thousand local and refugee Jews. Although they didn't kill the Jews there were instances when my family could have perished. One day, as the story goes, the people of the shtetl, including my family, were herded into the square for execution. Only the intervention of a high-ranking officer, who arrived at that moment, saved people from death. There was a legend that it was a Russian partisan in disguise.

In the spring of 1944, the Red Army pushed the Germans back to the western border of the pre-World War II Soviet Union. So, on March 17, 1944, the Red Army liberated Chechelnik. The Germans were too preoccupied, fleeing from the Russians, to think about the final solution. It was a miracle that my family survived and I had a chance at life. I was lucky. I was lucky in another regard too. While many of my friends and relatives were left without a father or with a father without a limb or two, I had both of my parents rather intact.

While Chechlnik's Jews survived the war, the town's Jewish flavour just made it for a few more years. By the time I left the Soviet Union, death, migration to cities, and emigration were already writing the final chapter of once Jewish shtetl. When I came to say goodbye to my place of birth and to the place where my ancestors were left behind, only about half a dozen old Jews remained there. Now, there are none in a once-thriving Jewish shtetl of many hundreds of people.

The Allied defeat of Nazi Germany accentuated the rupture between the Soviet Union and the United States that developed into the Cold War. When the Cold War began to blossom, I was old enough to comprehend that American imperialism was as bad as German Nazism as our propaganda bellowed to us. Just as one war ended, the authorities already were preparing us for another. I remember the drills during my school years where we rehearsed what to do in case of a nuclear attack. We hid under our desks. We also learned how to put a gas mask on in case of a chemical attack. As we were preparing to defend our Fatherland from American imperialists and believed we would defeat them as we did the Germans, the same drills, I learned later, were running in American schools.

Steadfast though they seemed, my beliefs in the communist propaganda didn't survive for long. The first crack, although hidden, came from the singling out of Jews. I didn't connect anti-Semitism with the Soviet regime until my late teen years. Still a true young communist, I just began to wonder how such an ugly thing as anti-Semitism had still existed in such a beautiful country. Whenever they called me a Zhid, it chipped quite a few of my beliefs away. And it happened often. After learning that I'm a Zhid for the first time in the first grade, people often reminded me of that. Many events sank into my subconscious; others had a profound impact on me. Two events would begin to change my view of my country. In these two events, I was not just in words but in the flesh attacked just because I was Jewish.

Chapter 5

One day, after my fifth-grade classes were over, I started down one of the only two unevenly paved roads in town that led to my house. My mood was great. No school tomorrow, most of the homework I did in school, an 'A' on a math test, and *The Three Musketeers* book awaiting me. What could be better than having a great book in one hand, a piece of bread with butter in another, and the warm oven wall behind me?

Two older boys appeared from the side road. As I stared at them, my heart began pounding. I looked around, there were no people on the street. I quickened my steps. Too late to run from them. They accosted me. Without saying a word, one hit me in the face hard. So hard that I saw stars. Inwardly, I writhed in agony. *Would he hit me again? What should I do? Run? Scream? Fight?* I didn't scream, though my world shook, slanted, and turned over. But I didn't fall to my knees. I just stepped back with a silent "Why?" in my eyes. The other boy shouted "Zhid!" as if answering. They casually walked away, the one who hit me paused for a narrow appraising glance over his shoulder. I, at a snail's pace, continued home. On the way home, I tried to come up with a reason for those boys' hatred. What immediately popped into my head is what I just learned from our history teacher the other day about the Nazi's hatred of the Jews.

More than six decades later, I still remember the boy's last name, *Chaliy*. I wish I could forget it. I remember every thought that ran through my mind at that moment, and my face starts to burn when I think about it as if it just happened. At that moment, something inside me died, and it never grew back. After all those years, I remember it all. Even now that it was only a memory, the feeling of helplessness and humiliation stays with me like the glow of a burned wood under the ashes. I wish I fought back, but I was too shocked and afraid.

When I returned home, the warm whiff of bread baking in the brick oven and the sight of my mother cleaning the kitchen filled me with a sense of security. "I made you a *butter bread*—a Russian name for an open-faced sandwich—have it now with milk. When papa will return from the Shabbat prayer, we will have dinner later."

"Thank you, mama." I took the sandwich and a glass of milk, and, keeping my face from her, sat by the warm wall. My eyes glazed unseeing at the book, my head throbbing, and my cheek burned from the hit. The other cheek burned from humiliation. I took a sip of the milk. Drops of milk slid along the side of the glass as I set it down. I didn't turn the page for a long time, and after a while, I was the D'Artagnan beating the hell out of Chaliy until the noise from the kitchen brought me back from the dream. I felt better.

Forward six years, another boy attacked me yet again just for being Jewish. Of course, I fought with other boys—we were boys after all—but it wasn't about my birth identity.

It was December 30, the last day before the winter break. The school let us out earlier. On this sunny day, my Jewish friend Leonid and I walked out of our tenth-grade classes. The snow was sparkling, the air was crisp, with eleven days of bliss ahead of us, we were in high spirits.

"What are you doing during the break?" said Leonid.

"Nothing special, maybe my parents will throw a birthday party for me. Do you remember it's on January 9? Any particular plans for you?"

"No, just relax."

"I think we will spend most of the time together, save reading." Reading aside, what else could we do; a movie just on weekends and no other entertainment in a small provincial town.

As we approached Leonid's house, a boy ran towards us. I didn't have time to be frightened, his wide-open eyes and mouth caused me automatically to turn away. He stabbed me in the shoulder with a pocket knife and sprinted away screaming. The raw hatred in the boy's face when he shouted Zhid scared me more than the knife. He couldn't come up with such hatred on his own. He stabbed me with the hate he inherited from the long line of his ancestors.

My eyes wide open, I looked at my friend. *What for? Could he have killed me?* I saw my fear reflected in Leonid's eyes. I still could feel my dread from that day. Physical wounds heal, but psychological ones last forever. With this event years in the rear-view mirror, I still remember the boy's last name, *Buchatskiy*. I don't carry him with me. I carry my scars. I see that some such events were more telling than others, but they were always about hatred.

"What should we do? Go to the clinic? Go home? What?"

"Let's go to my house and see the damage," said Leonid. His parents were at work; my mother stayed at home.

We went to his house. I tried to unbutton my coat. Leonid helped me. After removing the coat, I looked at him.

"There's no blood," he said. I exhaled and took off my sweater.

"I'm not sure."

When I unbuttoned my shirt and bared my shoulder, Leonid said, "I think the blade was small and your winter coat thick so it barely broke the skin. There is just a little blood." A tentative smile twisted my lips.

"What should we do?" I said, relieved that my parents wouldn't notice anything.

"It's small. Why make trouble for your parents?" I kept on looking at him.

"What?"—he said—"Do you assume they would go to the police?" He confirmed my thinking. Jews just kept their heads down to avoid any trouble.

I never sought the fights I had as a Jew, but they seemed to find me. These and other not as dramatic events weren't entirely unexpected. Something in my schoolmates' whispers and looks was distantly familiar to what I saw in Buchatskiy's amplified through the whole ten years of school. It felt to me that I not entirely belonged. They played with me, they talked with me, but I wasn't one of them. I was different—a Zhid. I was in the country, but somehow not of it. Just by the chance of my birth into a Jewish family, I was not truly a part of the country I was born in. If a child is born in America, he or she is an American, if a Jewish child is born in Russia or Ukraine, he is not Russian or Ukrainian, he is Jewish—a small and persecuted minority.

Though I was never again physically attacked because of my identity, there were other ways to emphasize that I was different, hated, and not welcomed in this land.

In long food lines at stores, we heard:

"You people are always trying to sneak in."

Or, "They aren't used to staying in a line like everybody else."

And years later, "Go to Israel where you wouldn't have to stay in lines."

Nobody wondered who the mysterious 'they' or 'you' were. During my Soviet years, I had to stay a lot in lines. Standing in lines for bread, milk, or kielbasa, I felt the gaze of people running down my nose, along with the implied question "Why didn't you move to Israel already?" As a child, my parents from time to time woke me up at four in the morning to wait for bread delivery. As an adult, I waited in lines to provide basic necessities for my family. As a potential emigrant, I had to stay in line every weekend to confirm my place in the line to submit my papers to the dreaded OVIR (department of visas and permissions). Scarcity accompanied every Soviet citizen, save the nomenclature, every step of the way from the cradle to the grave. Growing up both belonging and not belonging was hard. The dichotomy was difficult to live with even as an adult, but doublethink was the condition of life. To survive, most of us had two lives. Strangely, life felt simple; you sliced your soul in half—one half for salespeople, teachers, and officials, and the other half for your private life with family and friends. But even your private life, to a large extent, was formed—that is deformed—by the Soviet system.

Chapter 6

For me as a young boy, it was a struggle to fill in the gap between what we were taught to believe about communism's high ideals and the anti-Semitism I had encountered. Life was a struggle between reality and illusion. At this time, the high ideals won, but I still felt like I wanted to find a few answers. Written materials on Jewish culture and Jewish history were for the most part inaccessible when I was growing up. Snippets of information could be found through oral information from people who, despite the risks, were willing to help fill in the gap. Sorry to say, I didn't ask a lot of questions while the people who could answer them were alive. We were discouraged to ask questions. I wish I had been more inquisitive and learned more details about my parents' lives and the lives of my ancestors. But adults, by and large, were reluctant to talk about certain things, either because they didn't know the answers or, often, because they were afraid of repercussions. Only seldom and mostly by accident would they let down their guard enough for us to learn a bit beyond the official version of events.

The only adult willing to explain some, but not all, things to us was my friend Leonid's father, Yakov, my namesake. I called him Uncle Yasha. He became the figure of authority to me after a few instances when I realized that he was knowledgeable and willing to talk to us. One time I remember we had an argument with Leonid about how to spell the word accumulator, Russian for a battery. I said that the letter that goes after the double 'c' was an 'a' and Leonid said it was 'o'.

"Let's go and ask my father," Leonid said. "He knows everything."

"It's 'u'," he said.

"Really, Uncle Yasha?" I gasped. "Or you just don't want any of us to be right?"

"Do you think I would lie to you?" he said. My cheeks got hot.

Another time, although I don't recall what we argued about and what the question was, I remember his answer, "Stalin is not the head of State. He is the leader of the Party; the head of State is Voroshilov, who is the chairman of the Presidium of the Supreme Soviet. Do you understand?"

I nodded, although I couldn't comprehend how anyone could be above our dear Vozhd. Uncle Yasha, was around forty, a dozen or more years younger than my father. He grew up after the revolution and received a better education. That's why—I rationalized—he knew more than my father. Despite the risks, he, sometimes, filled for us the gaps. Gaps that official history created.

On one occasion at Leonid's house, I said: "I've read a good book about the Ukrainian national hero Bogdan Khmelnytskiy."

"The hero?" Uncle Yasha's face turned red when he said: "Yes, he liberated Ukraine from Poland and reunited Ukraine with Russia in the 17th century. But, in the process, he decimated the Jewish population. It was a genocide."

"What is genocide?" That's how, little by little, we acquired bits of knowledge our educators kept from us.

"You can't find information on such things in official publications. By the way, don't believe everything you read. And please don't talk about this beyond these walls. But you can read about the treatment of Jews by the tsars," he said. "The authorities have no problems bashing the tsarist regime and emphasizing how the Bolshevik revolution improved the lives of Jews."

I was able to read about Catherine's the Great establishment of the Pale of Settlement which mandated where Jews were supposed to live. Later rulers put more restrictions and used Jews as scapegoats for many problems that Russia had at that time. They organized pogroms, redirecting the anger of the masses and allowing them to blow off steam by taking it out on Jews. Watch the *Fiddler on the Roof* to have an idea of a pogrom is—an organised massacre of an ethnic group, in particular of Jewish people in the Russian empire. When Russia's problems worsened, the problems of Jews worsened exponentially. 'Bei Zhidov, Spasay Rossiyu' (Crush the Yids, Save Russia) was a common slogan. I couldn't understand how this slogan survived in a communist society. But it did.

I first heard this slogan from a double amputee war veteran. When drunk, he dragged himself through the streets of the shtetl for hours. He didn't stagger because his legs ended just where his hips started. His crutches kept him straight. He said things we couldn't make sense of, but from time to time, he shouted out a few slogans clearly. His favourites were 'Long live comrade Stalin and Grisha

Gofman' and "Bei Zhidov, Spasay Rossiyu." Paradoxically, he was Jewish, and Grisha Gofman was his name.

When I asked Uncle Yasha why people wanted to crush the Jews, he said, "Not all people. You will understand it later." I heard this slogan over and over. It persevered until I left Russia and beyond.

Chapter 7

I also read about how Jews had enthusiastically taken part in the Bolshevik Revolution in hopes that the new egalitarian social order might make their lives easier. At first, the new regime genuinely pursued a more egalitarian order. The country had become the world's first official anti-anti-Semitic state. The Pale of Settlement was dismantled and large numbers of Jews moved to big cities where they became instrumental in the development of the new state. The anti-Bolshevik forces used it to portray the revolution as a Jewish enterprise.

I wondered why my father didn't take part in the revolution. As he seldom talked about politics, I once dared to ask him: "Why didn't you partake in the revolution?"

"I did," he said. He was silent for so long I thought this was the only answer I would receive. The whole time, I stared at him waiting. He, at last, glanced at me.

"I was the first chairman of the local Soviet council in our shtetl," he said. "But quit during the Civil War that erupted after the revolution."

"Why!"

"Petlyura's troops killed the chairman of the Soviet council in the neighbouring shtetl of Obodovka by cracking his rib cage with a sledgehammer," he stopped for a moment and looked away. "I was afraid."

"Do you know who Petlyura was?" he asked.

"Yes, an anti-revolutionary."

"Not just that. He was a Ukrainian nationalist who in rebellion against the Bolsheviks blamed Jews for being both pro-revolutionary and pro-Russian." After a minute he added, "A Jew whose family was murdered by Petlyura's troops killed him in Paris, where he escaped to after the Civil War."

I felt good learning that Jews fought back but disappointed not understanding my father's decision to quit. Looking back, I think my father made the right choice. If he did survive the Civil War, he would have perished during the late

1930s purges when Stalin abruptly closed all Jewish schools and cultural establishments, and arrested and later killed many Yiddish writers. In that case, I would have never been born.

After WWII and Hitler's final solution, Stalin supported the creation of a Jewish state—Israel. But after it became evident that Israel had allied itself with the West instead of the Soviet Union as he expected, Stalin suspected that Soviet Jews were in secret working against the country. Soon after Hitler, the most notorious anti-Semite in history, dropped the sword of Jewish extermination, Stalin picked it up and raised it above the heads of survived Jews. He began his own anti-Semitic campaigns, beyond the anti-Semitism to a great extent amplified by Nazi occupation. Hitler had done it without pretences, trying to solve the Jewish problem physically. Stalin, more sophisticated, did it under the cover of what his twisted mind could come up with.

I was old enough to remember only his last campaign, the so-called 'Doctors Plot'. Without using the word Jew, the authorities printed the names of doctors who, they alleged, poisoned a few of Soviet leaders and even planned to poison our beloved Vozhd comrade Stalin. Nine of the twelve names sounded Jewish, but that didn't mean the other three were not Jewish. I remember the anxious whispers of adults, the firing of our neighbour, a Jew, who was a special investigator in the local prosecutor's office. I recall one day, when my father, who worked out of town, didn't come for Shabbat the anxiety felt by my whole family.

"Mama, why everyone is so scared?"

"Do you remember how you've been called this ugly word for the first time?" I shrugged. "Do you remember when a boy called you Zhid and hit you just because of that?"

"Yeah, so what?"

"Adults do the same in times like these. Maybe they have beaten your father or, God forbid, worse happened," she said with a surprising bitterness.

"What do you mean in times like these?"

"Go and read your newspaper. Maybe you will find the answers."

Puzzled, I went and picked up the newspaper I was obligated to subscribe to as an aspiring Young Pioneer. It was the *Pioneer's Pravda*. When I finished reading what I thought was a relevant article, I asked my mother, "What is cosmopolitan?"

"I don't know," she answered. And that was that.

By now, I knew where to find my answer. Next time, at Leonid's house, I ~~asked his father~~ "Uncle Yasha, what is cosmopolitan?"

~~"A cosmopolitan is a~~ citizen of the world. Like people who are loyal not to the country they live in but to the whole world."

"So, who are the cosmopolitans in our country?"

"In our country, we don't single out any group. Everyone is equal in our country. But under the guise of combat against the cosmopolitans, they really mean Jewish intellectuals. Not Jewish workers though."

At that time, I didn't understand what he meant. But decades later, in the United States, when I heard a member of the Trump administration called the outgoing chief economic advisor, Gary Cohn, a 'globalist', I didn't need to ask what being a globalist meant. I even tried to find out if cosmopolitan and globalist were synonyms. What I found out, like the word cosmopolitan, globalist was a moniker that many saw as anti-Semitic. When Ann Coulter clarified that it implied Jews and her followers on Facebook put comments like 'Paul Newman is a half globalist', and 'Jack Tapper is a globalist', I was appalled.

In the NRA director Wayne LaPierre's speech to a CPAC, he blamed Soros, Bloomberg, and Steyer—three Jewish billionaires—for financing the anti-gun movement. He held responsible socialists for pushing for gun control and named two other Jews—Karl Marx and Bernie Sanders. He never said the word, Jew. Maybe I was oversensitive, but it sounded alarmingly familiar. The difference was in this country statements like that weren't state-supported.

Being a Jewish doctor—Jewish anything, really—in those days signified all but certain doom. During Stalin's final months, the accelerated campaign of anti-Semitism made Jews afraid of their futures. There was something untenable about their lives—from quotas of Jews allowed at universities to primitive hatred that came from ethnic Slavs to outright worry about survival.

I didn't understand the severity of the situation we were in until much later when I learned about Stalin's plans. He allegedly intended to hang the doctors publicly and, after that, to 'save' the Jews from people's outrage. When a state says something, its citizens take note. Although it has never been proven, there is evidence that he planned to use these plots to justify the deportation of the entire Jewish population to Birobidzhan, a desolate region in Siberia that had been established after the revolution as the Jewish Autonomous Region. They say authorities already prepared trains equipped with cattle cars near the major cities where most Jews lived. A lot would die on the way to the far corner of Siberia, and more after they reached the inhospitable destination in the wilderness. The persecution of Jews by the Soviet government and fellow citizens was well known, and Jewish life in the country was one of discrimination, at best, and physical danger.

Chapter 8

They say Lord works in mysterious ways. Maybe God felt guilty for letting the Nazis get away with the Holocaust and lent us a hand this time by ending Stalin's rule.

But at that time, Stalin's death stunned me as it did most of the country. For me, Stalin was a symbol, a secular god, a word from a verse we had repeated often. "Thank you, comrade Stalin, for our happy childhood." His image permeated my early school years always plastered in the Young Pioneers newspaper. He looked magnificent with his determined face, wise eyes, and the uniform of a Generalissimo—the equivalent of a six-star general. I couldn't comprehend how a 'god' could have died from a stroke.

I remember that day. It was a dim morning on March 5, 1953. The radio played symphonic and chamber music in a sad minor key, instead of telling how many tons of grain and steel our heroic peasants and workers produced. Even after all these years, I still hear the familiar baritone of Yuri Levitan broadcasting the news of Stalin's death. He was a Jew, who made the most important announcements since the beginning of the Great Patriotic War due to his booming voice. Outside the post office, where the loudspeaker hung from an electrical pole, I broke into tears. Most people did. Some people just stayed motionless, tears running down their faces. Others hugged or otherwise comforted each other, and also cried. They cried because of real sorrow or feeling helpless having no rational way of predicting what would happen to them. One man surprised me; he was crying, but his face wasn't sad. They all cried because they sensed that, for better or for worse, an era had passed. Our Vozhd gone, the nation became fatherless. I came home to sad parents rubbing their puffy red eyes.

"How we will live without Stalin?" My eyes welled again when I said his name. They both glanced at me.

"There will be changes," my father said. "There will be changes."

My mother hugged me, and I sobbed in her embrace.

After the initial shock of Stalin's death, the general atmosphere in the country lightened, and the danger to the physical existence of Soviet Jewry appeared to have ended. Nikita Khrushchev was elected to the crucial post of General Secretary, and right away after Stalin's death Lavrentiy Beria brought to an end the 'Doctors Plot' investigation and released the doctors who didn't yet die from torture. In the summer after Stalin's death, many things happened that I didn't understand. Beria, the powerful member of the Politburo and head of Stalin's secret police—the predecessor of the KGB—was arrested. The newspapers ran stories that accused him of drinking, womanizing, and spying for the British. *How could it be?* His portrait was removed from my classroom. One of my friends said, "Let's go to the store to see if his portrait is still there." We ran to the store. The picture was gone. We just looked at each other. In December of that year, he was executed.

December of 1953 was cold, but the political climate was warming. The climate lightened enough for two letters from my father's sisters, who emigrated to Mexico and Argentina, to break through the Iron Curtain. But my father was afraid to answer those letters and that was the end of the communication. Thankfully, he kept the letters, and my sister didn't throw them away after he died. I didn't care about the letters, but three decades later they played a vital role in the future of my family.

In the mid-fifties, I was still a good pioneer and a strong believer in communism. But a few events had occurred that sowed seeds of future disillusionment. And invisible cracks portended the eventual demise of my beliefs. The cracks widened when I learned about Khrushchev's epochal 'secret' speech he gave at the XX Congress of the Communist Party denouncing the cult of Stalin. In essence, he said that the leader I had been taught to worship as the 'Father of the peoples' was a genocidal tyrant. When the information was out, it shocked the nation. For a twelve years old boy, it was confusing and difficult to stomach. I no longer knew just what to believe in. All I could do was look at my idol collapsing before my eyes, like the captain, I saw in a war movie, helplessly watched his ship slipping beneath the waves. Neither my parents nor the teachers explained what happened.

A year later, after another fight in the Central Committee of the Communist Party about denouncing Stalin's cult of personality, news circulated that three senior members of Politburo conspired to remove Khrushchev from the post of the General Secretary. They lost, were expelled from the Party, and pronounced an anti-Party group. I was not yet analytical and did take the information at its face value, but these events brought the dam holding beliefs they infused me with close to collapsing.

Consolidating his power, Khrushchev initiated some changes. Those changes somewhat liberalized the regime and became known as 'The Thaw'. Eventually, Khrushchev became an autocrat. He must've been an intelligent guy to win all power battles with other members of the Politburo. But he was poorly educated and made a lot of uninformed and impulsive decisions. And we know what happens to a country when a uniformed and impulsive person makes voluntary decisions. In 1959 Khrushchev went to America and discovered corn on the cob. He later introduced corn as a magic crop that would feed Soviet cattle. We were to catch up and leave behind the United States in the production of meat and milk. 'Dognat I Peregnat' (catch up and overtake) in dairy and meat production was the slogan of the day. It became ridiculous after a while. Regular people on the street had their idea about the slogan. "We'd better not overtake," went a popular wisecrack, "or the Yanks will see our bare asses." People called Khrushchev—Kukuruznik (Corn Man) because he had crowned the alien corn 'the new Tsarina of the Russian fields'. The corn that did so well in America didn't like Russia's cold weather. It was a bad call not only for the country but for Khrushchev's political career as well. Lack of know-how and Russian climate made the whole corn adventure a disaster. It was one of those impulsive and poorly thought-through decisions that his enemies cited when they later removed him from power.

Chapter 9

Although after Stalin's death I was ready to die for his cause, as time passed, I liked the parades and the rituals less. Still a good pioneer, I looked forward to joining Komsomol, the Young Communist League, at fourteen and exchanging the red tie for a Komsomol badge with Lenin's profile on it. At that time, I didn't know about Bar Mitzvah, but strangely, both, in their way, symbolized entering adolescence. The difference was that my grandchildren studied for their Bat/Bar Mitzvahs the Tora, I studied the Communist Manifesto. In 1958, I proudly joined the Komsomol organization.

Joining the communist youth organizations was not in theory mandatory, but in my entire childhood, I heard of no one daring to refuse to join. We all anxiously looked forward to it. Years later, in the early 1970s, as a teacher, I came across a few brave students who refused to join them. They were rare exceptions. I asked one why he hadn't joined Komsomol.

"How would it benefit me?" he said and looked at me as if it was so obvious. I was silent, thinking.

"This in terms of benefits. I was proud of becoming a member of All-Union Lenin Communist Union of Youth, Komsomol, for short."

Another milestone for me was receiving my passport that the state required everyone over age sixteen to have. The only people without passports were peasants who like their serf ancestors could never leave their villages. Holding it in my hands, I felt like a grown-up. I opened the passport: my first name was on the first lane, my patronymic was on the second one, my last name was the third, my date of birth on the fourth, and my 'nationality' on the fifth line stated Jew. I didn't question why the passport had the fifth lane. I had to adopt the established 'nationality' of my parents. On my birth certificate, they both were designated as Jews. Jewishness was defined in strictly ethnical terms. Religion had no place in building the Radiant Future—Jew was an ethnicity or a nationality, as they called in Russian, not a religion. The significance of the fifth lane I realized later.

The remaining school years were mostly uneventful, save one event right before my graduation. It cemented my view on the personal and institutional anti-Semitism in the country.

At the end of the tenth grade, the final year of high school, for an offense I don't even remember, I and two of my classmates were told to summon our parents to see the principal. Of course, we didn't tell our parents, hoping that it will blow over. For three days, we were not allowed to attend classes. On the fourth day, they announced that we were expelled from school. That's when I said that I didn't respect our principal. We had no choice but to tell our parents.

"How could you say that you respect the principal as your chemistry teacher (in Russia principals taught a few classes) and don't respect him as a principal," my father said after meeting with the principal.

"But that's true."

"It doesn't matter. Never talk about your superiors this way. There are consequences."

And consequences there were. I learned the lesson my father wanted me to live by: you're the boss, I'm stupid; I'm the boss, and you are stupid. People who grew up in the Soviet Union harboured fear for the perceived authority.

I had been a candidate for a silver medal given to students with mostly 'A's. On the final math exam, my favourite subject, I received my third B and was deprived of my deserved medal. It was by design. I was not sure if it was personal for the principal or it was from above not to award the only medal in school to a Jew. After that, it got worse. I needed a letter of recommendation for the college admission application without which one couldn't take the college entrance exam. The principal refused to issue the letter. No matter who lobbied on my behalf, he refused. "This Jew needs to be taught a lesson," he told one teacher who happened to be my cousin's husband and an ethnic Ukrainian. I was sixteen and a half and bewildered. *How could he do that to me?*

Only two days before the deadline, when the principal left for vacation, an assistant principal signed the letter. My sister had to rush it to Odessa by overnight train trip.

Everyone knew, that getting into a prestigious university, where admission was in theory based on test scores, was all but impossible for a Jewish kid, however talented. And the more modest colleges had unofficial admission quotas for Jews; different for different majors. Math, science, and engineering were popular college majors for Jews and more accepting of them. Getting into medical or pharmacy school for Jews was virtually impossible. So mostly, they didn't even try. Soviet authorities denied the existence of state-sponsored anti-Semitism. It meant nothing. They denied many other obvious things. For example, that they would fail exam takers on purpose.

The 1950s came to an end for me in August of 1960 when I moved to the city of Odessa. They ended for me by imprinting in my brain and soul that I was not a Russian by nationality and religion, but a Jew, even though the latter notion had no precise content or connotation. Although a Russian-by-culture, I was a Jew-by-birth. Still a good Young Communist but wiser, I've learned two important lessons, one from my father and one from my non-Jewish compatriots.

The decade ended with me trying to figure out how the best country in the world tolerated rampant anti-Semitism. With each discovery and each anti-Semitic event, my feeling that I didn't belong grew. Not realizing it, I was ready to begin changing my unconditional belief in the communist system. I just needed a trigger.

Part II
The Country Is Different

Chapter 10

A significant chapter of my life began when I moved to the city of Odessa on the Black Sea from a small shtetl. On the face of things, not much had changed in the world around me since I left the rural fields of Southern Ukraine for Odessa's urban jungle, but the 1960s played a big role in changing my perception of my country and the world.

In August of 1960, four months shy of seventeen, I passed the entrance exams and gained access to the Teacher College of Odessa. I had no desire to become a teacher at this time, but the higher academic institutions to become lawyers, doctors, diplomats, and even military academies, were not realistic opportunities for me as a Jew. Even in average universities, only math and engineering professions were more or less open to Jews. Because not many aspired to be teachers of math or physics, it was easier for a rural Jew with limited educational opportunities to be accepted, and I loved physics.

Tuition was free, and textbooks I borrowed from a library. And if students were in good academic standing, they received a stipend. Like most out-of-town students, I was granted a place in a dormitory for a symbolic fee. With a little help from my parents, I didn't have to worry about money. One of the great things of the Soviet era was free education.

Settling down in the dormitory, familiarizing myself with the college, and getting books from the library took the whole week. I hardly left the campus and didn't have the opportunity to explore the city life when we were sent for about a month to a collective farm to help with harvesting. This form of servitude was a common experience of college students and urban professionals. We picked corn, tomatoes, and potatoes by hand throughout September. We lived in a huge barn equipped with bunk beds. All the amenities were outside. It wasn't a problem for me. I lived my whole life like that, and the outhouse in early fall wasn't as bad as in winter.

The diverse student body was a new experience for me, and I soaked in the novel environment. It was a lot to absorb. I needed guidance which I found from two native Odessa guys, Misha and Tolya. They became my friends, and I followed them everywhere. I spent most of the time with them and acquired the nickname of *khvostik* (little tail). Misha, a Jew, was an intellectual. He was not just intelligent; he was also cultured. Tolya was gentile and street smart. They both, in different ways, were typical natives of Odessa.

In October, upon returning after harvesting, we, at last, began studying. Besides my studies, I spent most of my free time away from the dormitory. I wanted to learn about the city and city life. The urban life left an immediate, lasting impression on me since Odessa was such a glamorous and original city with its architecture, ambiance, and local colourful dialect. The city, far removed from the shtetl in many regards, was a big move for me. The transition from a small town with its inhabitants with a simple outlook to a big multi-ethnic, multicultural city with an educated and sophisticated populace began changing my worldview. I learned there so much. But what I learned dwarfed by what I couldn't.

When you come from a shtetl like Chechelnik, you discover how you compared to the new world out there and realize what you were missing all your life. From the first day, I was enchanted by the city and wished I were born in Odessa, a city of diversity, sophistication, and wit. Odessa would have infected my soul the day I was born. It would have left a permanent mark on my personality. But I was not to be born there. We can't choose where, when, and to whom we were born. If we were lucky, we were born in the right place. If we were not, we struggled to right the wrong. Odessa began to reshape me, as I began to reshape my life. There was a lot to absorb for a shy shtetl boy and, if possible, to catch up. Odessa became a really important part of who I became, but the shaping years were mostly behind me. It would take a lot of effort and years to change. You shape your life and your life shapes you. As they say, you can take a boy from a shtetl, but you can't take the shtetl out of a boy. I tried to blend in, but I couldn't. It was obvious that I was a small-town boy dealing with teens from the city. I was a kid and wanted to fit in. Could I do it without help?

Chapter 11

One day, instead of going to the dormitory, I went with Misha who walked to his home. When we were in a park, I asked Misha, "Would you guide me in exploring city life?"

"Of course, no problem." I looked at him with anticipation. "Start with Privoz. There's a saying that Odessa begins with Privoz," he said. "We, Odessa natives, regard it as the heart of the city. Privoz market," he explained, "is one of the biggest, if not the biggest, in Europe. But it is famous not only because of that. You will see it for yourself, and I'm sure you will appreciate it."

"So, you will you go with me?"

"Uhm… I'm not sure," Misha said. "If I have time. If not, go on your own. It's an opportunity for you to meet authentic Odessa-type people and authentic food and see the tapestry of demographics, hear the colourful language, and experience the local kind of wit."

"So, you won't go with me…" I bent my head. We walked for a while in silence.

"You know," Misha said, "I have a few minutes right now. Let me give you a little history lesson."

We sat down on a bench, and he began, "To create such a jewel as Odessa, it took a different kind of people to contribute." He fell silent for a moment.

"First, a German, whom you know as Catherine the Great—"

"She was German?"

"Yes. You didn't know?" I said nothing.

"She realized the strategic importance of a port and a naval base on the Black Sea for Russia. She chose a place and ordered to build a fort. That's how our city began."

"They say there was a statue of Catherine in this square," I said.

"Yes, there was. And there was a cathedral here also. Both were destroyed after the Bolshevik revolution."

After a pause, "That's why this place is still, despite the authorities changed its name, called by the people Sobornaya Ploshchad, or Soborka for short." Sobornaya Ploshchad means The Cathedral Square.

"Then, there was the Duke de Richelieu, a refugee of the French revolution. He became a godfather of the modern city. In Odessa, he is known as just the Duke."

"Why did they allow his statue to remain intact?" I asked.

"I don't know."

So, there are some things he doesn't know.

"Greeks, who came here, connected the city with the Eastern Mediterranean." he continued. "Adventurers from Italy poured into the new city and gave it their lightness, musicality, and architecture. From the start of Odessa, Jews engaged in retail trade and crafts." He felt silent, and I waited for him to continue.

"Descendants of Ancient Greece, Rome, and Judea—the creators of Western Civilization—built the city. Odessa, like the Babylon Tower, was built by different tribes—great peoples."

"What about others?" I asked.

"And, of course, the Russians who were the rulers of the city, and Ukrainians—the sailors and masons. Everyone contributed to the character, culture, and language of the city."

Babylon Tower of Odessa

What a lecture. He knows a lot and enjoys lecturing. Right there he stopped and stood up. "Okay, I have to be home in a few minutes," he pointed to a beautiful building across the street. "I live in here."

"What day is best to go there? And what time?" I looked up at him.

"Sunday is the best time. Not too early and not too late." He extended his hand.

I stood up and I shook his hand, not letting it go for a while.

"You know," he said, "if you can come here at about 10:30 on Sunday, and wait till eleven I'll try to go with you. If I'm not here by eleven, go by yourself." I let go of his hand.

I couldn't wait till Sunday. I woke up with anticipation and walked the few blocks to the square arriving half an hour early. The cool morning air was crisp, and the smell was sweet and fragrant. I found a bench in front of the building where Misha lived and sat down facing it. The square was festive with fall colours of yellow, orange, red, and green. The fall mornings in Odessa were sweet and dreamy with the spicy scent of acacia. The clear sky promised a beautiful day. I tilted my head and was lost in dreams.

"Let's take the tram to Privoz." Misha appeared from nowhere.

As we entered the tram and settled down, the conductor hollered, "And so, who is riding in my tram without a ticket." Typical Odessa. When she announced 'Privoz', we got off and entered the market.

Chapter 12

The market encompassed a few city-blocks and had open-air stalls and pavilions built in the pre-revolutionary times. Here, I found a true cornucopia: from potatoes to pomegranates, from oxtails to live chicken, from fish to shrimp. In the dairy pavilion, the countertops are filled with milk and kefir, feta cheese and farmer cheese, butter and sour cream. I have never seen such an abundance of food anywhere. The colours, the smells, and the noise made me gaping.

"Wait until you taste the food. Let's start with the produce section," Misha said, seeing my reaction.

I looked around surprised by the mixture of people in the market. Plump Ukrainian women from the surrounding villages spoke a lively mixture of Russian and Ukrainian. People from Moldova and the Caucuses sold grapes, watermelons, and oranges complementing local vendors. Gypsy women with small children roamed through the thick crowd begging and holding on to people, and gypsy men sold black market stuff while looking for the opportunity to trick people. My ears listened as people spoke broken Russian with distinct sentence structures and accents.

Local sellers had a real sense of humour. A sign on one of the stalls, "Don't massage tomatoes!"

I heard, "Stop touching my cucumbers. They won't get any bigger and harder like you know what."

"Did you hear that?" I became excited.

"I heard. That's what I was talking about," Misha said.

"Will I fit here?"

"Reeba, Reeba, Reeba," A sudden shout: Reeba was the Odessa version of the word ryba, which meant fish. The English version would be 'feesh'.

"Oh yeah, let's go to the fish section. Local women sell there the gifts of the sea Odessa is famous for. You will hear the most interesting conversations there."

We didn't have comedy clubs in the Soviet Union, but it was the closest thing to it. There you could hear uncensored jokes and witness hilarious situations. I overheard an exchange between an old Jewish lady and a fish seller:

-Your feesh fresh?

-Sure. You not see it's alive?

-Oy vey, I'm alive. So what?

Located on the Black Sea, Odessa was a major port, and the seafood trade was one of the main industries. There you could find a wide variety of fresh, smoked, and dried fish, along with shrimp, mussels, and sardines.

And, of course, Privoz inspired a lot of seafood *anekdot*s.

-Buy some fresh fish, sir!

-Is it really fresh?

-What a question! Just came out of the sea.

-Why are its eyes closed? Is it sleeping? And why does it stink like that?

-You want to say you can control yourself while sleeping?

In the meat pavilion, there was an abundant selection of products: buzhenina (chewy cold baked pork), vetchina (Russian ham), home-made kielbasa with real meat in it. In state stores, they said, kielbasa had paper and other fillers in it to account for the stolen meat. And the aromas. Thankfully, the smell was free.

"Whatever you buy," Misha said, "always bargain, you'd upset the seller if you didn't. And you'd miss a price you can afford. Godly food, but an ungodly price, as we say."

It was good advice. Later on, I liked to come here to taste products I could never see in state stores and couldn't afford for a long time; and, of course, to listen.

Jewish butchers, with tongues as sharp as their knives.

"Give me a kilo of meat without bones."

"Without bones? Drek is without bones. Meat has bones. Drek is the Yiddish word for crap."

"Listen, Misha, I'm falling in love with Odessa. Thank you." I said.

"Ah, Odessa, the pearl by the sea, goes the famous song," he said. "But wait until you see the rest."

"Let me tell you," he continued as we walked through the market. I walked as if in a dream. "A lot of humour originated in Odessa. Our ability to turn any dialog into humour is famous all over the country. The city became the humour capital of Russia."

The world didn't know about the uniqueness of Odessa, but when the Iron Curtain became porous and next disappeared altogether, the city became famous all over the world. When listening to great comedians here in the United States, I can make a compelling argument that the style of modern Jewish-American humour, from Jerry Seinfeld to Larry David, stems from Odessa, with its disturbed and gloomy flavour. When I watch *The Larry David show*, I become nostalgic—for the city, not the country. Odessa has a long tradition of unique, quirky (mostly Jewish) local jokes. The city's greatest wits were Jewish and so were the fiddlers, writers, and Mafiosi. By the way, George Gershwin, Bob Dylan, Joe Dassin, and Steven Spielberg are a few Americans with Jewish Odessa roots.

"Let's continue the history lesson," Misha said. "With its checkered demographics, Odessa was a thriving melting pot of Greeks, Italians, Russians, Ukrainians, and Jews. The street names reflected the diversity: the French Blvd, Italian Blvd., Greek St., and Jewish St."

"I didn't see these streets. Where are they?"

"Oh, the Bolsheviks renamed a lot of streets after famous communists. Besides Marx and Lenin, only historians remember who they were."

After the fall of the Soviet Union, most of the streets would be renamed to their original versions.

"What about Stalin Street?" I asked.

"It was renamed again after the denouncement of his personality cult." He looked at me and said, "We Odessans are more open-minded than people in most other parts of the country."

"I'm open-minded."

"Not as much as we are. We've been in contact with many ethnicities, religions, and cultures for more than two centuries."

He enjoys lecturing.

"Even our faces look different from the rest of the country."

"Thank you," I said. "So not only am I a close-minded shtetl boy, but my face is backward too?"

"Uhm… that's not what I mean. All I'm saying is that in Odessa, the culture is different. Even the way we speak Russian is different."

"So, again, I don't fit."

Misha continued as if he didn't hear. "We even produced our version of Russian with a particular distinction that earned it the 'Odessan yazyk (tongue) designation'." I guess I looked puzzled because he explained, "Our Russian is influenced by different languages, especially by Yiddish intonations, grammar, and idioms." After a pause, he said as if offering an apology, "It will be easy for you to adapt to. And your face will fit."

"Yes, the language sounds familiar," I said with a smile.

"Nehama, make night," Misha smiled.

"What's nehama?"

"Nehama is a Jewish female name. It's strange that you don't know."

Is he again hints at my shtetleness?

"Anyway, this phrase, from a story by the famous Odessa-born genius writer Isaac Babel," Misha smiled, "gives a feel of how they spoke in old Odessa."

"By the way," he added, "I very much recommend you to read Babel."

"I never heard the name."

"You are not alone. After Babel was executed in the late 1930s, his books were banned and destroyed. Only recently a provincial publishing house put out a limited edition of his stories, and—"

"Where can I find the book?" I interrupted the lecture.

"Not so fast." My disappointment must've been all over my face. "Maybe I could help you," he said. "We will see."

"Certain words you would hear only in Odessa. Only in Odessa, we have *sininkie* (the little blue ones), the local name for eggplants. Only in Odessa, the first course of a dinner, that in Russia is a soup or a borsht, is called *zhidkoe* (liquid)."

I recalled the first time I heard the word from my aunt Sonya admonishing us, citing Russian wisdom: "You have to eat *zhidkoe* every day, it's healthy for your stomach, and you must eat it with bread. You won't have constipation, and bread will fill you up."

It was good advice. When I didn't have enough money for a full dinner, I went to the campus cafeteria and bought half a portion of borsht. Bread and mustard were free on the tables, so I spread mustard over bread and filled myself up. I still like to eat this way while struggling to limit bread consumption.

Misha assured me that everybody develops a special relationship with the city, especially if one lives his life there. I absorbed every word, and, after the excursion, devoted many hours learning about the city, at times with friends or relatives and at times alone—watching, listening, even touching. Odessa became my city. The city is the only thing I miss about the old country. Though it is now Ukrainian politically and geographically, it never was truly Ukrainian. After the Bolshevik revolution, Odessa and the whole South-East of modern Ukraine, like later Crimea, which never belonged to Ukraine, were assigned to Ukraine. The Bolsheviks thought that the Soviet Union would be forever and it didn't matter to which part any of the territories administratively belonged. The result of this thinking was highlighted during the Crimea conflict in 2014.

When the majority of Jews and other minorities left, the city changed dramatically—ethnically, demographically, and culturally, and not for the best. The local language became as dead as Latin; especially when the authorities tried to force Ukrainian on the mostly Russian-speaking population. Only those who write about old Odessa still use this variation of Russian and will always use it to bring readers into a specific time and context.

You still may catch the past, not in Odessa though but in Brooklyn's Brighton Beach. Some of old Odessa was preserved there when in the 1970s thousands of Odessa Jews immigrated to the area, establishing a 'little Odessa' frozen in the Soviet past. They tried to recreate the old life there instead of building a new one.

Chapter 13

In Odessa, I was introduced to *anekdots*. Whenever I will use Soviet anecdotes, and I will use them often, I will use this spelling. An *anekdot*, unlike anecdote, is a *fictionalized* short story with a *punch line*, often politically subversive. It has to be like lingerie—short, intriguing, and rather fresh. *Anekdots* were more than just funny stories, for they often had a message for the listener. First, you laugh; next, against your will, you all of a sudden fell silent and thoughtful.

It was hard for many Soviet citizens even to understand how bad the regime was. Political conditions in the Soviet Union were responsible for the unique humour produced there that helped people, who didn't believe the propaganda but were not brave enough to explicitly express their views, vented their frustration. Communism's economic theories and system of repression created inherently amusing situations, a prolific humour-producing machine. Humour was one of the most effective ways of confronting adversity and coping with difficult situations, especially when we had little control over them or none at all. I loved to listen to and share *anekdots*, often perilous jokes that pushed the boundaries. They began the downhill fall of my love affair with Communism. Thanks to them I, at last, made a connection between anti-Semitism and the regime. Here is an example of a political *anekdot*:

A judge walks out of his chambers laughing his head off. A colleague approaches him and asks why he is laughing.
   – I just heard the funniest joke in the world.
   – Well, go ahead, tell me.
   – I can't; I just gave a man ten years for it.

And here are examples of typical Odessa *anekdots*:
   – "Lenin died, but his cause lives on." (An actual Soviet slogan)

– Rabinowitz notes: *"I would prefer that the other way around."*

– *"Comrade Rabinowitz, why weren't you present at the last open Communist Party meeting?"*

– *"Oy vey, no one told me it would be the **last** one. If I had known that, I would have come with my whole family."*

Rabinowitz, an old sly Odessa Jew, was the central fictional figure of countless *aneckdots*, a brunt of Odessa Jewish jokes. Lion Feuchtwanger, the famous Jewish-German writer, said, "By its taste and reality Jewish humour reminds salt which we can't see because it dissolved in the food, but it's still there."

Now when only a small Jewish community remains in Odessa, they installed there a monument to the 'unknown Rabinowitz'. I like Odessa humour so much I can't help to tell one more *anekdot* a man, a virtual encyclopaedia of Odessa humour, once artfully told me. I still remember how he made a mini-performance of each.

"Have you heard this one?" His almond-shaped eyes sparkled. He raised his shoulder, crooked his mouth, closed one eye, and right away turned into the proverbial Rabinowitz.

-On Deribasovskaya street two women bumped into each other.

-Sara did you notice?

-No, what?

-I was in a beauty salon.

-And what…? It's closed?

If during my shtetl years I became pro-Jewish, the Odessa years, thanks in no small part to *anekdots*, were creating an anti-Soviet. Not yet ready to discard communism, and not even thinking of fleeing it.

Chapter 14

For the first time, thought about emigration occurred to me when, after a few months in the city, my father came to Odessa to check on me. It was the time of Khrushchev's rule when the authorities allowed limited tourism from the United States. So, an American, who after the revolution immigrated to the United States from our shtetl, was visiting Odessa at the same time. My father asked me to take him to the hotel where this man was staying. It was interesting for me to see an American. I had never had an opportunity to meet people from the 'rotten' West. And I had never had an opportunity to visit the hotel reserved for foreigners only. I was eager to see both and took my father to the trolleybus stop to get there as soon as possible.

"You know, the last time I visited Odessa was before World War II," my father said. "Let's walk. It's about a quarter of a century since I've been to a large city."

"No problem, I'll show you the most beautiful parts of the city. In the last few months, I walked those streets numerous times."

"Yeah, and I want to see the opera house. I remember how I enjoyed it the last time I was there."

"It's near the boulevard the hotel is on. We'll stop there."

We took the iconic Deribasovskaya street, the most famous in Odessa, and one of its symbols. We made our way through the straight streets of the old city.

"The buildings are beautiful," my father said, enjoying the historic architecture with a style more Mediterranean than Russian.

"Fortunately," I said, "most of the marvellous buildings that went up during the 18th and 19th centuries were not damaged during World War II."

We stopped and enjoyed the grand Renaissance-era theatre, regarded as one of the world's finest. They say the Odessa opera house is the second most beautiful in the world, after the Vienna one. It didn't occur to me that one day I would be able to judge it by myself. Passing the theatre, we entered the Seaside

Boulevard where the hotel occupied an elegant building. Entering the hotel built in pre-revolutionary times, we both froze in the lobby with our chins falling onto our chests. Two provincials amid luxury.

"Do you have any business being there?" A clerk brought us back to reality. He came across to me as a KGB man.

"Uhm… I… Uhm, we are," I said after a short delay, "here to see a relative." I looked at my father. "Barshefsky," he said the man's name.

The *clerk* went to talk to the manager. It seemed that it took forever. *Did I make a mistake coming here? Would I be in trouble at college?* At last, the clerk came back and barked, "It's suite 207," he pointed to the staircase. I exhaled and took my father by the elbow. The dark mahogany staircase was elegant and fit for a duke; its polished wood glowing in the soft light of a crystal chandelier. My fingers swept over the rich mahogany handrail as we ascended to the second floor.

I knocked on the door. As the door swung open, we saw a middle-aged neat well-dressed, and well-groomed man. He was no comparison to my father with his provincial Soviet attire and cheap haircut. The man looked younger, or my father looked older than their sixties.

They spoke Yiddish. When my father occasionally used a Russian word, the man inquired as if he had forgotten Russian or had never known it. My father knew no English. I couldn't follow the conversation completely because my Yiddish was limited. But I understood enough to think that the man made the right decision emigrating decades ago.

After we left the hotel, we walked silently, bustling along the boulevard. It was one of those cool Odessa days. The day was colder than it should have been in November. The sun just began its downward progress to the horizon. Babushkas and tourists on the benches took pleasure in the last partly sunny days of fall, enjoying the famous boulevard and seascape. For the people around, it was an ordinary day.

"What do you think," my father said.

"How old is he?"

"About the same age as me. Why, do you think he looks younger?"

I averted his gaze thinking it would hurt him if I said what I thought.

"When did he leave?"

"A few years after the revolution."

"Why didn't you emigrate?" I looked around to see if anyone from the hotel followed us.

"I was a well-to-do man and thought I had much to lose." He was silent for a moment. "Also, the Bolsheviks made it sound as if anti-Semitism would become a thing of the past."

I heard another emotion besides pride in his voice, therefore I asked, "Do you regret not leaving?" I passed the stage when I was afraid to question him.

He shrugged. "I don't know."

What if my future children will ask me the same question? What will be my answer? Should I think about emigration? It never before occurred to me that I want or be able to leave my country. As a Soviet citizen, I grew up in a world where no one talked about emigration. It was a taboo topic. So, the thought was gone as soon as it fully materialized zed. It was as if I glimpsed something, but it frightened me, and I erased it from my mind.

In the early 60s, there were no reasons for me to think about leaving. Despite the persecution of writers such as Pasternak, the author of *Doctor Zhivago*, Khrushchev's years were relatively free and became known as *The Thaw*. The government loosened the restraints on the culture, and people had hope for a positive change. With the appearance of the poetry of Joseph Brodsky, mostly underground, who was later persecuted and forced out of the county to eventually become a Nobel Prize winner and poet-laureate of the United States, and Yevgeniy Evtushenko, a popular poet, *The Thaw* continued. My student years coincided with relative cultural liberalization. I dreamed that righting the wrongs would open the full potential of socialism. But dreams don't linger, they dissolve like rising smoke from a chimney. All that is left is a sobering reality. *Will the Thaw last?* The thought lingered in the back of my mind.

Chapter 15

Stepping on campus one morning, in the late fall of 1961, was like entering a different world. I had never seen so many people with grim faces in one place since Stalin's death. They assembled in small groups talking and looking around. *What happened? Did some big shot die?*

"He's a f...ing Jew-lover." I hurried away to another group.

"How did they allow this to be published? Was the censor asleep?"

I couldn't make sense of the remarks but was afraid to ask. I moved again.

"He slandered our people. He f...ing hates Ukrainians."

As the morning wore on, I searched for a familiar face to find out what's happening.

"Hey Misha, thank God. What's going on?"

"Have you slept through yesterday?"

"Don't ask me questions." I snapped. "Just tell me."

I probably could have handled it better.

"*Literaturnaya Gazeta,*" Misha said after a short delay, "published Yevgeniy Evtushenko's poem called *Babi Yar*. It's a bombshell."

Literaturnaya Gazeta, the extremely popular cultural and political literary newspaper with limited circulation, had the limited freedom to publish materials that didn't strictly follow the Party line. Evtushenko didn't always follow the party line either but didn't dare to deviate too far from it as Brodsky did.

"What's Babi Yar? I never heard about it. What's it about?" When he didn't answer, I said: "Okay, I'll go and find the paper."

"Good Luck." He smiled.

I rushed to the college library.

"May I see yesterday's *Literaturnaya Gazeta*, please?"

"Are you kidding, there's a line of a few dozen people. I doubt you can see it today, or ever," the librarian said.

I skipped classes and went into the city to find the paper. In a couple of libraries, I had the same bad luck. I went to a newspaper stand, but the lady just gave me a look as if I were crazy. On the stand were only official voices of authorities—*Pravda (The Truth), Izvestia (The News), and Trud (Labour).* There was a joke—a newspaper salesman yells, "The last *News*, No *Truth*, only *Labour* remains." *Pravda* didn't exist to tell the truth but to distort it. *Izvestia* didn't exist to distribute the news but rather twist it to fit the regime's goals. Kind like Fake News. *Trud* didn't exist to protect working people's rights but talked about our heroic workers and peasants.

After a few hours of racing through the city, I got a hold of the newspaper and read the poem. Perplexed, I began to read it again. *How did they allow this to be published?* I wondered how the chief editor of *Literaturnaya Gazeta* cheated the censors. It was the first poem about Jews I have ever read. It was the first time I have read something sympathetic towards Jews. It was confusing, with the unknown facts and unfamiliar names like Dreyfus and Anne Frank.

The poem dealt with the 1941 German slaughter of tens of thousands of Jews in the ravine (yar) outside Kiev, the capital of Ukraine. The ravine was called 'Babi Yar'. It appeared that the Soviets were, at last, acknowledging the unique dark destiny of the Jews in their midst, who were lost to the cruel hatred of the Nazis and Ukrainian anti-Semites. Till now they kept it a secret because part of the local Ukrainian population was as guilty of the tragedy as the Nazis were. Now, I understood the remarks I heard that morning.

The authorities almost right away regretted the publication, but couldn't unpublish the poem. The strongest proof of the poem's power was the ferocity with which the media tried to squash it. The papers were filled with denunciation and counter-poems commissioned by the Soviet authorities. In the underground publications called 'Samizdat' that meant self-publishing where you don't need a dash for 'without government's permission'—counter-counter-poems appeared. In just a couple of weeks, the Ukrainian Academy of Sciences published a book called *Judaism without Embellishment.* To denounce the poem, they filled the book with ugly racial cartoons reminiscent of Nazi propaganda.

Not often, the poem changes the way a nation remembers history. Yevtushenko's *Babi Yar* did. For me, it was a time of reckoning with what humans are capable of. So many souls had disappeared into this yar, it was difficult to comprehend its magnitude. All that remained of them were the facts Soviet authorities kept hidden.

Many things that were exciting and confusing happened in the early 1960s when the Khrushchev's Thaw continued. Later this year, Stalin's corpse had been evicted from Lenin's mausoleum on Red Square. It was buried in secrecy near the Kremlin wall.

The theatres were, for the first time, screening Hollywood films. I remember *The Magnificent Seven, Sun Valley Serenade,* and *Twelve Angry Man.* The last one had a big impact on me. People, not the authorities, can decide the fate of a man? It was shocking.

At the end of 1962, Solzhenitsyn's account of life in Soviet labour camps called GULAG, *One Day in the Life of Ivan Denisovich,* appeared in the literary journal *Noviy Mir (New World).* Khrushchev in person approved the uncensored publication about Stalin's GULAG. People who read it were shell-shocked. It became a sensation not only inside the country but outside. It was almost impossible to get a copy of this book. I had to reserve it and read it in the library since they didn't allow taking the book out because of the demand. I fidgeted and bit my lips many times while reading. *In Soviet camps? We are not Nazis.*

The novella wasn't large and I read it in a few hours. The content of the book was a stunning revelation to most Soviet people. Many did not believe it. I hardly could believe it also. The very fact of the publication has sent an intriguing signal. Things were changing.

Still, many things remained the same. One of them was elections. On January 9, 1962, I reached the voting age of 18. The next election was scheduled for February. Despite my hopes that the country was changing for the best, I wanted to protest the elections. Only one candidate, the one appointed by the Party, was on the ballot. We could vote only for one candidate the same way we could buy only one brand of vodka, 'Moskvskaya'. It was not an election but a selection. Not voting wasn't an option. When I entered the voting place, I took off my 'ushanka' fur hat, received the ballots, and instead of putting them in the box I hid the ballots in the hat and walked out. I felt good.

Years later, when I was forced to participate in the comedy of elections as an official—the authorities made me an agitator, a 'volunteer' precinct worker—I laughed at my youthful naiveté. My job was to bring the voters from an assigned multiunit apartment building. Since there was just one candidate, the agitators spent little time talking about elections. Instead, we talked about the importance of voting.

"Don't worry, Yakov Isaakovich," people assured me before every election, "we will be at the precinct before noon." The building was near my school where the precinct was located, so people knew me. No agitator could leave the precinct until everyone in his assigned building had voted. Anyway, at the end of the day, we would put almost all of the remaining ballots in so that the candidate would be elected with 99.99% of the vote.

Odessa taught me that I live in a country different from the one I knew before. There, the seeds of doubt found a fertile environment. My beliefs—survivors of my first real-life encounters with anti-Semitism—began to fall apart. For me and many of the young people, who were born during or after World War II and who came of age in the post-Stalin years, dissatisfaction with the regime took the form of listening and dancing to Western rock music, wearing jeans, if we could afford to buy them on the black market, and trying to dress in styles imitative of American young people. The State greatly disapproved of people who did it. Soviet propaganda invented the derogative word for them—stylyagy, a derivative of style. In the media and Komsomol youth meetings, the stylyagy were criticized and denounced.

One must be blind to the gap between theory and practice. There were many blind, or maybe it's better to say blinded people in the country. I wasn't as blind as I was before, but still, the rosy glasses of Soviet propaganda distorted reality. I thought if we can correct the wrongs, socialism still can be mankind's future. I was growing up and changing, but slowly.

Chapter 16

During my college years, some pivotal experiences changed me. Of course, every experience changes you, but a few do it to a great degree. Two events stood out and made me realize that I had to change when life unfolded itself to me peeling away its layers piece by piece. Transformation is a journey, and two of the most fateful events happened while I was traveling. One was a bus ride.

It was late August. I cannot be more specific, for little did I know that that day would affect my entire life. I was about nineteen at that time. I remember walking to the bus that would take me to the village where, because of the shortage of teachers in rural areas, for a year, I would start my new life as a paid student-teacher. After a year I would come back to finish my shortened education. I felt rich and grown-up. I was almost running as I thought about my own money and, more or less, stopped when thinking about crazy middle school brats. "Am I a man already?" I thought. Nineteen was a strange age to be—not a boy, not a man yet that I aspired to be.

The sun was shining, a little low in the last days of summer. With extreme heat memory and the days bright with just an occasional cloud in the southern blue sky, I anticipated a relaxing ride.

I jumped onto the step of a small, once yellow bus. Even under the mild morning sun, the packed bus felt hot. The passengers, mostly misshapen older women in colourful kerchiefs that allowed telling apart their sunburned faces, talked quietly. They paid little attention to me. It suited me well. I smiled and looked for a seat. My smile froze as soon as I noticed a young girl on the left side towards the rear, by the window. She appeared small in stature, with black hair that fell about her childlike face. There was no one next to her, the only free seat. My seat. The darkness, as if a cloud covered the sun, ran over the sudden silence.

You would think that at my age I would become even more excited; not me. Young unfamiliar girls terrified me. I never spoke to girls whom I didn't know for as long as I could remember. They seemed to glue my lips together so even

Hercules couldn't take them apart. My spine straightened as if someone barked "at attention," and my neck became inflexible. Without looking at anyone, the smile still glued to my face, I dragged myself to my seat. Without bending my back, I lowered myself into it, putting a thoughtful expression on my face. I looked straight ahead and hoped that my face conveyed my deep and smart thoughts. But that was not what was running through my head.

I am a grown-up.
You are a shmock! When will it stop? Why can't I talk to her?
Why am I agonizing?
Oh God, why are you punishing me?
Do something.
What? Now!

It felt as if a cold soundproof glass was between me and the girl. I closed my eyes in the hope darkness would give me relief and courage. I practiced in my mind.

- *Hi, I'm Yakov. What's your name?*
- *Maria, nice to meet you, Maria.*
- *Where are you going?*
- *What brings you there?*
- *Well, it's been nice talking to you.*

I opened my eyes; my mouth didn't follow the lead. For what looked like a long time, I continued telling myself that the next moment the rehearsed words would come out of my mouth, but my subconscious had already decided that it wouldn't happen. Even if by magic my lips moved apart, I wasn't sure the girl knew her part of the script. I tried to see her without turning my head, thinking she might think I was sneaking a look at her, but all I could see was a hill, framed by the window. A few hours later, the arrival at my destination was a God-sent gift. Like before, I dragged myself the whole length of the bus to the door that promised reprieve. Self-pity tore my heart to pieces. *A man who allows himself to be nothing has no place in this world.* Feeling as if I had been put through a meat grinder, I lowered myself off the bus that pulled into a dirt-filled plaza off the paved road. The moving bus kicked up a flume of dust.

It smelled of the countryside that even the smell of the overheated engine and dust behind the bus couldn't spoil. I took a deep breath, the first in a long time, and inhaled a sun-coloured day. The air was pure and the heavens deep. A quick look around. A small convenience store. A woman with a hand on her belly bulged sideways approached the bus. A young man with an untucked shirt followed her. It was still summertime, and the late afternoon sun was hot. The full weight of autumn was yet to come. The sunlight turned to gold the dust. The wind blew through the treetops, and they bent forward as if forced to their knees.

Out of the blue, as if guided by an outer force, I walked along the bus to the last window. The girl in the window frame reminded me of a picture by a famous Russian painter Levitan. Without thinking, I raised a hand in a sign of farewell and this diffident, almost shy gesture had an unexpected effect on me. Magically, my lips moved apart saying goodbye. As if waiting for this, she waved back, a shy smile touched her lips. The sun became even brighter and birds sang louder.

What a day! A day of hot sun, of serene air, of deep skies; a day of consequence. That day was the beginning of something I could barely define. Something that I felt would be difficult, wrenching, but necessary.

"My God!" I pondered. "I had screwed up before, but failure had never bitten so deep. I have to change." I started down the street on a journey from boy to man, from student to teacher.

Student teaching was uneventful. The only thing I remember vividly was the assassination of President Kennedy. The youthful president was popular among many Soviet people. His death was a blow to our hope that the relationship between the Soviet Union and the United States could improve. A question we discussed was: "How a country could allow its president to be killed?" And, of course, the worry about what the change in the leadership of the Superpower will bring to the world.

Talking about the change of leadership, the political death of Nikita Khrushchev, the leader of the other Superpower, made us worry not only about that but about what will happen to the Thaw. Things were going bad for Khrushchev. After a stretch of prodigious economic boom and scientific achievements peaked with a man in space, his career belly-flopped. After the 'kukuruza' debacle, the bungled Cuban missile crisis, and the Virgin Lands' scheme of planting corn en masse on the Central Asian steppes that ended in disaster, the country and the country's leadership were ripe for a change.

After teaching for a year, it was another one at the college. I have graduated from the Teacher College In 1965. Because higher education was free, we were required for three years to work where the authorities sent us. Because of the shortage of teachers in rural areas, I was assigned to a remote village. The system determined what one could study, where one could work, and where one could live. We were told that we would receive our diplomas after one year of working where we were sent. To sweeten the exile, the Teacher's Union, we were automatically members of, offered a free two-day cruise. I had never been on one before, so I took the cruise. Things weren't completely bad: a free cruise, free education, and free health care, but no free speech, no free movement, and no free information. Besides the novelty, the cruise was an opportunity to hone my developing skills to handle unfamiliar girls.

The cruise played a vital role in my transformation as the bus ride did.

Chapter 17

We boarded the ship at around 1 P.M. A June sun hung above the harbour and coated everything with blinding shine. The air smelled of paint and rotten fish. Small green waves raced from the ship to the wharf.

A crew member directed us down to our cabin. A lot of people might be bothered by it being on the last deck down, windowless, and with two beds down and two beds up. Not me. My new bunkmates and I fast decided who would sleep were. I put my luggage in the closet and went to explore the ship.

I went to the upper deck and stood there, eyes wide and staring into the sea. Everything was new to me and interesting. I found out that the ship was built in the 1930s in Germany and taken by the Soviets as reparation after the victory in World War II. We renamed it *Victory*. I wandered around for an hour before ending up on the upper deck where I settled into a faded white chair. The wood slats nearly broke under me, armrests rusted. We didn't take good care of the ship since Germany lost her. I reclined against the beautiful robin's-egg blue of the summer afternoon; a beautiful view of the city, a light breeze, and a salty miracle of sea and sun. Life was good.

"Let's go and have a drink," my roommate, Ivan, approached me.

"Why only one?" I stood up.

We went to find a bar. After a few drinks that put fire on and loosened my tongue, life became even better. The youthful bus ride played in my mind. Although I was working on overcoming my shyness, I was not there yet. Alcohol did the rest. Shyness had gone; I was in my element: free, confident, and ready to conquer the world. I loved the world and held it in my heart. A young girl went by.

"Nice dress," I said.

"There is nothing under it." Ivan grinned.

"There is a *great deal* under it." That fetched another grin.

"Ivan, let's go to the main deck to find girls," I suggested.

"No, I need more drinks."

"Alone?"

"If you are leaving, I'll find someone else." He waved his hand.

I skipped steps capturing the peeled-painted rails. At the main desk, I bumped into Peter, a fellow student.

"Let's have a drink," he suggested.

"Oh, I had a few just now and they went right to my head." With disappointment on his red face, Peter left me alone.

I looked around. Music, colourful dresses, loud conversations, and laughter added to the anticipation of a great evening. There were a lot of women, young and old. Everyone above thirty was old. A girl by the window in a white linen dress with ash-gold hair against the blue sea looked at the city. She caught my eye. Under the influence of vodka and anticipation, I approached. I caught her scent before I saw her face.

"Nice view." I said, "May I sit here?" *It's not the girl on the bus.* The drinks helped.

She turned and flashed a quick look, the sun lighted up beautiful green eyes. She looked down and shrugged, "Sure, why not?"

It seemed she needed help too. I sat down inhaling the subtle smell of her perfume.

"Thank you. I'm Yakov. And what's your name?"

"I'm Laura."

"*Ni*ce to meet you, Laura, are you a local?"

"No." she took a quick look out the window. "I'm from Sebastopol."

"Oh, the pride of Russian sailors. So, you are going back home to Crimea." When she nodded, I asked, "Did you enjoy Odessa?"

"It's a wonderful city; such rich architecture. The Opera House is the jewel," Laura said.

I looked out the window too and moved closer pointing at the boulevard. Our knees banged against each other. Laura moved away but not too far.

"Look at the Primorsky (Seaside) Blvd, isn't it lovely?"

Babushkas parked on the benches and cracking sunflower seeds, iconic granite Potemkin steps that lead from the boulevard to the sea, and the Duke statue—a real duke who escaped the French revolution—the city's mayor credited splendid emergence of this city known as Sothern Palmyra or Odessa-Mama to its inhabitants.

A waiter approached, "Something to drink?"

"May I buy you a drink?" I looked at Laura.

"Umm… Yes." Laura shrugged again while touching her hair.

When the waiter brought the drinks, I was looking into the front of Laura's dress as she bent forward to accept the glass.

We drank and talked more until the drinks required me to take a break. I excused myself and hurried to the bathroom looking forward to a nice evening. When I came back, I noticed an older man seized my seat and was talking to Laura. I twisted my mouth and was not sure what to do. My right hand tightened into a fist. I wanted to go over and take this guy and knock the hell out of him, only I knew I wouldn't. What I lacked in height I compensated with a direct gaze and squared shoulders as I walked to the table. My throat tightened as I crossed my arms over my chest, first one and then another.

"By the way, I know karate," I bent approaching the table. Even now, I don't understand why I said this. I was disappointed in myself; I should have been smarter.

"I respect people who know how to defend themselves," the man stood up and extended his hand. "I am Igor."

The expression on his broad-boned face with a slight cleft in the chin was friendly.

"I am Yakov," I shook his hand after a short delay.

"Yakov, are you angry at me?"

"Why?"

"I just sat down to enjoy the view. If you don't mind, I'll sit here for a few more minutes."

He asked a few questions. Learning that I am a newly minted teacher, he said that he was a school principal from the Ural region. He was old, but not enough to be a principal.

"You are surprised that at thirty-five I'm a principal. You may become one too," he said looking at me.

Not with my Jewish baggage.

After a few minutes, he said goodbye, and I had Laura to myself.

We continued to talk. I ordered another drink. While toasting, our hands touched and came apart like branches of trees in the wind. She agreed to show me her city, and we arranged to meet after she would drop off her luggage. We danced, went to the upper deck, kissed, and danced again. We had a good time. At about six A.M., after we kissed goodbye, I went to the upper deck. I needed fresh air. The morning sun's rays, unobstructed by any buildings or trees, painted the sky burnt orange. A light breeze cooled me down. I looked around. Igor was there.

"Yakov," he said. He pulled a chair up close. "Sit down."

With care, I lowered myself into the seat and said, "Why are you so early up?"

"Just wanted to see the sunrise over the sea. Isn't it beautiful?"

After so many years, I don't remember everything we talked about. I fumbled my way through small talk punctuated by uncomfortable silence. But when the conversation became political, I became agitated. He compared Stalin with Hitler and the Soviet Union with Nazi Germany. At first, I had shaken his words off as instinctively as a dog shakes off water.

"Why won't you admit?" He eloquently began to make his case. "The National-Socialist Party in Germany and the Communist Party here were the only ones allowed." He emphasized "socialist."

"Yeah, but…" In the silence between his words, I furrowed my brows while trying to find what to say back.

He continued. "If this is not enough, the Fuhrer and the Vozhd at the top, the KGB and Gestapo."

"Yeah, but…" The same thing happened.

"Add the concentration camps and the Gulag camps."

My possible answers made me uncomfortable. It occurred to me that maybe I didn't understand what happened during those years. He was light-years ahead of me in understanding Communism's true nature. As Igor was speaking, I thought, "It can't be right." I struggled to find counter-arguments, but couldn't. The first line of adulthood vacillated across my forehead. I crossed my arms just about convinced.

As we parted, I uncrossed my arms and after we shook hands wrapped them around myself. I never would have thought that one conversation could change my views, and it didn't completely. Belatedly, I found a counter-argument, "In words, if not deeds, the Communists, unlike Nazis, weren't overtly anti-Semitic, racist, and homophobic. They didn't slaughter people for *these* reasons." Although I accepted everything Igor said, I sensed I would never see the past and future events the same way as before. On that morning, the way things appeared to me, changed forever. The main lesson I learned was that interpretation of events was just that, interpretation. From then on, I didn't see any issue in black-and-white, only in innumerable shades of grey.

It was another day I would never forget. Why the transition from boyhood to manhood was happening to me while I was traveling? You change only when you move?

After the cruise, it was to the village for a newly minted teacher who had more questions than answers.

Chapter 18

In the village, the school, the local Soviet office, and a small convenience store with about empty shelves were the only attractions. There were no paved roads. I was advised to buy knee-high boots to be able to navigate around. *It's not Siberia, why I feel I'm exiled?* I was cut off from the people who understood more than what newspapers printed.

One day, newspapers brought bad news. There were articles about the arrest in September 1965 of two Soviet writers Yuli Daniel, a Jew, and his friend Andrei Sinyavsky, whose works had been banned in the Soviet Union. They had several of their manuscripts smuggled out and published abroad. The detention, coming a year after the sudden ouster of Khrushchev, signalled that the new leadership of the country decided to tighten the screws. Is the *Thaw* over? The Party began an extensive and brutal campaign, condemning the two writers for their slanders of the Soviet society. The arrest caught the attention of the world. Foreign stations broadcasted news of the KGB action. When my landlords were not home, they let me use their short-wave radio. I tried to make sense of what's going on. There was no one to discuss the situation with.

One morning, in the teacher's planning room, one teacher said holding a newspaper in her hands, "Having read everything they wrote in the newspaper about Daniel and Sinyavsky, I'm profoundly convinced that they hate the Soviet people."

"But you haven't read their work," I said.

"I haven't read any of it, nor do I want to. There are quotations in the papers that prove it and it's enough for me."

What the paper wrote was a lie. That lie had been the people's, who believed the authorities, truth.

"You can take any quotation from Marx or Lenin and prove anything."

Certain words are just better left unsaid. I more often than not realized it right after I said the words. A wise man once said... nothing.

After one year of working in the village, I needed *a kharakteristica* to receive my diploma. It was a letter of recommendation vouching for my character and loyalty to the State. At the meeting where they discussed the matter, the principal said, "We won't report what you said about the Daniel and Sinyavsky trial. We don't want to destroy your career. But be careful in the future."

The trial was the beginning of the end of the Thaw. The Kremlin followed this trial with a long and determined crackdown on dissidents and unofficial publications. I began to sense the weight and darkness of the place in which I lived.

After I brought the *kharakteristika* to the college, they finally issued my diploma. Diploma in my possession, I tried to obtain permission to live in Odessa and find a job there. I failed at both. Without a stamp in my passport allowing me to live in Odessa, I had no chance to find a job there. It was another year in exile. But this time I would have my consolation prize. A big one. Great events turn on small hinges.

One evening in mid-October, I attended a dance party for students hosted by the school. While we were standing in the lobby, an elderly woman and a young girl entered. The principal met them and they talked for a while. I looked at the girl. Brunette wavy hair framed the tanned oval face with brown eyes and full lips. She wasn't skinny, just as I liked. *Who is she? What is she doing here?*

I took a quick look at the assistant principal who stood next to me.

"This is your future wife," he said, poking me with his elbow and eyeing the girl. I hardly diverted my eyes from the girl either and shot another quizzical glance at him. His protruding stomach gave a real workout for the buttons of his shirt. He winked at me and explained: "The girl will be teaching German. Her name is Emilia." Mila for short, I learned later.

"She is too young to be a teacher," I said.

"We don't have a foreign language teacher from the beginning of the school year. And we are not the only rural school in this position, so the regional department of education allowed the graduates of a special school in Odessa where a lot of subjects were taught in German to fill out teacher's positions in remote villages. She just graduated."

"Do you think being just about the age of her students and nice-looking too she is up to the task?"

"So, here is an opportunity for you. Become her mentor." It was an interesting suggestion.

Although I didn't pay attention to his remark, it was prophetic. She would be my wife for forty-seven years and not full two months.

I looked at the girl as the principal led both women to his apartment in the school building. I wished she would look at me but ended up taking in the curves of her body under the tight sweater. She had pretty legs, and the way she swayed her hips made my heart forget a couple of beats. She made her home in my heart before she settled in my head. On my way home, I hoped my life would become exciting.

After we were introduced the next day, seeing her in school every day wasn't enough. I invented reasons to see her as much as I could.

"If you'd like, I can help you with lesson plans." At least I had a college behind me and more than a year of teaching experience.

"Yes, it would be great."

We began to write lesson plans together. It seemed she felt as lonely as I was. I showed her where the store was, brought her to the library, and invited her to a movie that they showed here at weekends. We also taught the evening school a couple of days a week. One night, seeing her off after school, I pointed upward.

"Can you find Venus?" The night sky, a dark mixture of blue and purple, was beset with stars. The stars seemed so close they could almost be touched. The dark sky and the brightness of multiple stars created a perception of infinity.

"It's beautiful," Mila said after a minute of silence. "It looks like someone took a handful of sparkles and just threw it up to the sky. The sky is never like that in Odessa." After a long moment, "How can you find a specific star when the sky is sprinkled with throbbing diamonds?"

"Venus is the brightest star. And by the way, it's a planet, not a star." I took her by the elbow and pointed out the brightest diamond in a diamonded sky.

"Look here," Mila pointed towards the northern sky.

I looked up, still holding her by the arm. "This is the Northern Star, it guided men for millennia."

We talked a lot. I did most of the talking. After all, I had a college behind me and I wanted to impress her. I told her things I've never shared with anyone, and she wanted to hear more. She was a great listener and inquisitive.

"Why didn't you get a job in Odessa?" Mila asked.

"I don't have permission to live in Odessa. Besides, the country requires I work here first three years after receiving a free education." After a pause, I said, "I wonder what brought *you* here of your own free will."

"It's been my dream to study German at the University. But I'm Jewish. Teaching German in a rural area may help, at least to study by distant learning."

I wasn't sure when it happened or when it started, but seeing her became important to me. I thought she enjoyed my company similarly but wasn't sure if she felt the same. I was determined to make her care about me. Over the next few months, we spent a lot of time together. Love is a blessed feeling. It's like a hurricane born over warm waters that grow to huge strength. In favourable conditions, the strength of it doesn't abate.

In late winter, Mila and I got married. We didn't plan to get married, at least not yet. I'm not sure how it happened—neither of us officially proposed or anything dramatic like this. One evening we spoke about marriage in general.

"Do you want to get married?" I asked. I was twenty-three and she was nineteen.

"Is this a proposal?"

"Yes. Why not?" I brought her hand to my lips. She swallowed. I pressed my lips to her hand again. Her eyes were moist.

The next morning, we asked the principal and he arranged with the local Soviet for us to be married the same day. The principal and assistant principal's families together with my landlord arranged a party. That was our wedding. Looking back on what brought us to this moment, everything appears predestined—a series of coincidences leading us right to this. There were a million ways it might have gone differently.

The remaining months of the school years were the happiest in my life. I didn't read, didn't listen to the 'enemy voices', and the time flew by. But even in the happiest times, some things make you worry. The 1967 Six-Day War between Israel and three Arab states was such an event. In the first couple of days, the Soviet media portrayed the war as a win for the Arabs. The destruction of the Jewish state terrified me. I spent evenings glued to the short-wave radio.

"Why do you listen so much to the radio?" Mila said. I heard the frustration in her voice.

"Should the Arabs succeed in destroying the Jewish State, where Jews would go if, God forbid, there was another Holocaust."

On the third day, the news from the 'enemy voices' diverged from the Soviet ones. The war ended with a decisive and surprising rout of the three Arab countries that, armed to the teeth by the Soviet Union, expected a quick victory and the solution to the Israeli problem.

"I'm so proud that Jews proved they could fight, despite what people here say." I shared the news with Mila. She didn't say anything.

"If you think it doesn't concern you, see what would happen." I continued. "Authorities will find a way to blame the Jews for the failure of Soviet weaponry and advisors. Don't think that it wouldn't affect you and your dreams."

Sure enough, in retaliation, the Soviets unleashed a vicious anti-Zionist campaign that not only Jews but all people saw for what it was. In the months that followed, Soviet authorities identified Zionism as a crime and equated it with allegiance to a foreign country. It wasn't subtle, and it unleashed a wave of nasty anti-Semitism in the country.

The Six-Day War had one effect on Soviet leadership. It had quite a different effect on Soviet Jews. Before the war, few Jews, if any, immigrated to Israel. Israel's decisive victory changed the opinion of many of them towards Israel. Following the war, a few began applying for exit visas and demonstrating for their right to move to Israel. At first, they were religious Jews. But the victory catalysed a revival of national consciousness among the majority of Jews, which in turn unleashed a movement for free emigration to Israel. The mainstream of Soviet Jews was afraid to express their opinion. I was among them. But it is insane people who make things happen. In Moscow, a few courageous souls began to demonstrate demanding the right to immigrate to Israel. They were arrested and exiled from Moscow. But their actions made headlines around the world and unleashed the 'Let my people go' movement of American Jewry. The doors of the Soviet Union might never have been opened for mass Jewish migration was it not for the courageous and active minority of Soviet Jews and Western support. The pride for the Jewish State and the anti-Israel campaign—a great disguise for growing anti-Semitism—and courageous actions of the few made me consider possibilities that the door out of the country for Jews may be open. I shared these thoughts with Mila.

"Mila," I said. "There is a state where we would be accepted as Jews, and be safe."

"Are you talking about emigrating?"

"Not emigrating, just talking about it."

"No sane person," she said, "would oppose the Party and the State and risk everything. And the security situation there? Don't ever talk about it."

"You see," I said to Mila. "I'm not the only one considering the possibility of emigration."

"And where did they end up? Do you want to go to prison? And what about me?"

She was right. It's wonderful to think about what you wish for. It's difficult to live by that. There are many reasons why, such as KGB and GULAG. She was smart, I thought. I had a woman to hold dear and care for. To hell with all dissatisfaction. So, I stopped talking about emigration, but I couldn't stop thinking about it.

Ten months after we married, my daughter Rika was born. I was overjoyed. That took the thoughts about emigration completely out of consideration. I stopped thinking about politics. Taking care of my family consumed all my time.

I stopped thinking about politics, but politics didn't stop causing changes. Humiliated, the Soviet leaders even considered military intervention in the Israeli-Arab conflict, but the development in their own backyard took it out of consideration. The new leadership of the Czechoslovak Communist Party tried reforming the Soviet brand of socialism and talked about 'socialism with a human face'. Soviet leaders saw this undertaking as a greater threat to the system than developments in the Middle East. The Soviet society, at first in small numbers, started to split away from the Bolshevik brand of communism. The overwhelming majority of Soviet people were not opponents of socialism. They just longed for changes. But our rigid leaders thought differently.

Next year, things happened that put thoughts about emigration back on my agenda. The Czechoslovak experiment had to be stopped. On August 21, 1968, Soviet troops invaded the country and put an end to the 'socialism with human face' experiment. Soviet troops rolled into Czechoslovakia, strangling the reform and, at the same time, helping to install a new Communist orthodoxy at home. Now each person had to choose between toeing the Party line to be allowed to advance professionally or put the career on hold while retaining decency and bidding their time until another thaw. For Jews, if they were not members of the Party or geniuses, the advancement almost didn't exist. As usual, there was a suitable *anekdot.*

In the Soviet time, a synagogue chooses a rabbi. There were three candidates: one knows the Talmud, but is not a member of the communist party; the second is a member of the communist party, but doesn't know the Talmud well; the third one knows the Talmud, is a member of the party, but is not Jewish.

You may guess who they chose.

The invasion marked the end of the *Thaw* during which young people began to lose their fear of sharing views, knowledge, beliefs, and questions. While sharing and questioning, most young men and women were still loyal citizens and no opponents of socialism. We wanted democracy, but it seemed more feasible for democracy in our country to evolve within a socialist framework. Like the Czechs, we embraced the 'socialism with a human face' idea. We hoped that the political and economic system Czechoslovakia's reformers were trying to create would be an example of socialism's evolution. But it was wishful thinking. Only a tiny minority, which became known as dissidents, fought for human rights—the right to emigrate among them. But the authority refused the requests to emigrate. In Russian, we had to invent a new word to describe the phenomenon. A few courageous souls, who applied for exit visas for Israel and had been refused, became known as 'otkazniks'. Because of the difference in culture, there wasn't an adequate word in English, and a new word that combined the English refuse (otkaz) and Russian word-ending 'nik' created the word "refusnik," as these people became known in the West. They were called this name not because they had refused anything, but because they had been refused permission to emigrate. Refusniks, especially the ones that went to prison, paid for their freedom in full. These pioneers, who finally were granted permission to leave, sent back word that life in the West was different, better, and freer. It offered opportunities to pursue happiness. As it's true of most social movements, the absolute number of activists on the front line was small, maybe a few thousand or less of the three million Soviet Jews. They pushed for the right to emigrate and risked the consequences of prison, thus inspiring what has been a silent majority to think about running off to the West. Later, people could escape with a discount, thanks to them. The movement did more than just inspire Jews. Soviet Jewry became a flashpoint in the Cold War. It went on being an issue John Kennedy ignored to an issue Ronald Reagan, decades later, put on par with arm controls.

The Kremlin response to the Jewish awakening was a hysterical anti-Semitic campaign thinly disguised as anti-Zionism. I still equate anti-Zionism with anti-Semitism.

As I matured, the reality of life began to erode the unconditional belief that I live in the best country in the world and that the Communism we were building was the pinnacle of human development. Thoughts that something wasn't right entered my consciousness. I held those thoughts to myself. Early in life, although not taught, we have learned to keep our thoughts to ourselves and function on two parallel levels at once: what we thought and what we told others. We all play roles in this world to survive and prosper. Now and then we behave in a way that does not make us proud.

At the end of the school year, we moved back to Odessa.

Chapter 19

In 1968 my father passed away. My deference from drafting into the army as the only child had expired (my half-siblings were out of the house for decades). I was drafted into the army. Because I had a higher education, it was only for one year. It occurred a short time after the invasion of Czechoslovakia. I was afraid that we could be sent there and of what could ensue. I recalled what one of my fellow students who entered the college after a three-year mandatory service in the army had revealed. He served with people who were sent to Hungary and witnessed the crashing of the anti-communist uprising there in 1956. They recalled that the Soviet troops were forbidden to use live ammunition. What the Soviets did, they attached gigantic chains to the tanks and drove them at high speed towards the protesters. Just before hitting them, the tanks made a sharp U-turn. The chains by inertia moved towards the crowd and cut the people like a scythe cuts the grass. Thankfully, my fear didn't materialize.

While in the army, a memorable thing happened. One day, the political commissar ordered me to his office. The first thought that came to my mind, "What's wrong?" All the way to headquarters I went over events of the last few days and still couldn't find the reason he called me in. As I approached the door to his office, I stopped and made fists. Before knocking at his door, I let out a heavy sigh. When he said, "Come in," I opened the door.

"Comrade lieutenant colonel, private Grinshpun at your order arrived," I said saluting.

"Relax soldier and sit down." He pointed to a guest chair.

I took the chair in front of his desk, leaning forward with my hands clasped firmly between my knees. He sat opposite, his gaze that of a school principal who wouldn't take a no for an answer. Above him, from the wall, Brezhnev looked at me without batting an eye.

"Are the soldiers in your unit treating you well?"

"Yes," I answered, of course.

"How is your family?"

I wondered what this is about, but what got the hairs on my neck to stiffen was his next question: "What do you think about the conflict between Israel and Arab countries?"

Caught off guard, I gave him the media talking points about Israeli aggression.

"Good," he said, satisfied with my answer. "Tomorrow we have an assembly condemning the Israeli aggression." I raised my eyebrows as he stopped for a moment. "I would like you to denounce the Zionist aggression."

"Are… you saying you want *me* to do it? I don't see how it's possible," I said, right away regretting it. "I am a Jew and—"

"That's exactly what I'm saying." He gave a brisk nod. There might be a smile on his lips, but it would be an equivalent to a frozen smirk. "It's important to show that *all* Soviet people condemn Israel. So…"

Not trusting my voice, I nodded as my shoulders slump. I had nothing to be ashamed of, but I was. Saying 'no' wasn't an option for me.

On the way back to the barracks, I looked down and away. I wanted to shriek or punch someone in the face. *Did I make the right decision? Could I answer differently? Would I have to lie again?* These thoughts swirled in my head. When it came to concealing my thoughts, I was not less capable than the next person. Although this was familiar turf—lies I had live before—I couldn't slander Israel and respect myself afterward. Agonizing till bedtime, I began to prepare my talking points. Without having a satisfactory speech, I plunged into an uneasy sleep. In the morning, I had a solution that, in my opinion, allowed me to appease the commissar and preserve my self-respect. I polished my speech and hoped I can execute it to everyone's satisfaction.

In the auditorium, sitting in the first row, I didn't want the meeting to begin and wished it was over. Tapping my fingers on the handles of the chair didn't speed up the time. When the commissar began to speak, I grasped the handles. I hoped he didn't see my white knuckles. His speech ended too soon. As I heard my name, I came to the podium. I looked at the fellow soldiers, then glanced at the commissar, and began talking.

"I denounce the Israeli cowardly attack at the brotherly Arab people. I hate the current Israeli government. But Israel was established to a large degree with the help of the Soviet Union. Stalin thought that the Labour party would turn the new country against the British imperialists and towards the Soviet Union. He even, through Czechoslovakia, supplied the new government with weaponry taken from the Germans. That allowed the new country to protect itself. Unfortunately, the subsequent governments turned Israel towards the imperialists. Again, I denounce the Israeli government and hope that Israeli people will sooner or later see who their true friends are."

Did the speech satisfy everyone? I didn't know, but I felt that I got out of the situation with minimum loss.

By the end of 1969, my mandatory service ended.

Part III
We Want a Different Life

Chapter 20

After leaving the army, I found a job and earned enough to afford my own shortwave radio. Shortwave radio broadcasts by the West were our single lifeline to the outside world. I, like many in the country, listened religiously to foreign radio broadcasts: The Voice of America, die Deutsche Welle (The German Wave), BBC, and Kol Israel (The Voice of Israel). The government called them "enemy voices."

The following *anekdot* underscores that a lot of people who didn't believe the official propaganda looked for information wherever they could find it, despite the danger.

A little boy cries in a store.

"Don't worry," the security guard says, "we'll announce on the radio for your parents to pick you up."

The boy stops, wipes his eyes, and sniffles. "Go on the Voice of America— that's all they listen to."

Listening to the broadcasts was like making a hole in the Iron Curtain. But as it was hard to make a hole in iron, it was difficult to listen to those broadcasts. It was an arduous job. Soviet law did not explicitly prohibit citizens from tuning in to foreign radio stations. Such a law would have been equal to acknowledging that they feared capitalist propaganda. The authorities tried to prevent reception by jamming broadcasts by producing a screen of noise the 'enemy voices' could not penetrate. They tried to keep the knowledge of other ways of life in the West away from everyone within its borders. However, jamming was costly and centred mainly on large cities. But even there it didn't entirely succeed. Usually, searching for about ten minutes, I could find a station that wasn't jammed completely.

"Why are you listening if it's so hard?" Mila said. "It could get you in trouble." She wasn't interested in the news.

"It helps to cope with the lies."

"Do you believe what you hear from the enemy voices?"

"I do. I believe everything as I don't believe anything our media feeds us."

"I don't. I think they don't tell the whole truth and I don't believe that don't say something that isn't true. It's propaganda." Soviets, generally, were cynical, especially when it came to the government and media.

"At least they don't lie all the time." I paused. "And what kind of a country would broadcast in such sordid details things like the Cuban crisis, Kennedy's assassination, and the Vietnam War. Only a free and strong country not afraid of the truth."

So, every evening, I went to the kitchen, the only other room in the apartment, closed the doors, and glued myself to the radio. I didn't want my daughter to disclose by chance, like the boy in the *anekdot*, that I listened to foreign broadcasting. I won't be sent to GULAG like during Stalin's rule, but I could lose my job or expect a talk with a KGB agent. We lived under the constant fear that the walls were listening. We knew the KGB watched us, they knew that we knew, and we knew that they knew that we knew. A miserable game, but we all played along. All of us pretended; the ones who watched and the ones being watched.

Learning of a different world beyond our borders, I had grown even more tired of the constant lies and censorship and the need to carefully watch everything I said. Learning of another life, it was still hard for me to understand how bad the Soviet regime was. I dreamed of changes and occasionally thought about emigration. That was all I could do. To fight the seemingly undefeatable state seemed pointless. The state had the power, we had desperation. I wasn't a hero, and I couldn't risk my job as a teacher. My family's wellbeing kept me from speaking out. Although I kept silent, the communism inside me was dying a difficult, smelly death.

To cope with the desperation, people found different means. Part of the intelligentsia found relief in 'internal emigration' to the kitchen table. Private life has always been the island of happiness in the sea of Soviet misery, and these conversations with friends and family have been a little warm pool of light in the totalitarian darkness. We tried to lose ourselves in the narrow circle of close friends and trusted acquaintants by exchanging and discussing what we heard.

In the pervasive atmosphere of fear and suspicion, the only people we could trust were our closest friends and, of course, the family. And every so often not even them. The following *anekdot* attests to that.

In GULAG, after a long day of hard work, the prisoners discussed the reasons they ended up there.

"I am here because of laziness," one man said.

"How come?" everyone looked at me.

"We exchanged political anekdots with my friend. When he left, I put my coat on to go to report to the KGB on him. I opened the door, and it was pouring outside. I decided against it. But my friend went, despite the rain."

Another man commented, "In the Soviet Union, there is freedom of speech. You may say whatever you want, but only once. It's not written anywhere that one should be free after that."

Others deliberately dulled their minds and concentrated on their careers. Soviet leaders and apparatchiks, Soviet dissidents and refuseniks, and people who just wanted to get out sat in the same classrooms and listened to the same communist wisdom, but have chosen different paths. The working class and peasants had their way of shunning the state, summed up in the words: "They pretend to pay us, we pretend to work." They and part of the intelligentsia who tried to find an antidote to spiritual emptiness drank themselves into numbing unconsciousness.

Once I asked a fellow teacher, a heavy drinker, "What, are you trying to find the answer at the bottom of the glass?"

"Vodka doesn't help to find the answer, but it helps forget the question." Amazing answer.

Vodka became a great psychotherapist. By the age of eighteen, everyone in the Soviet Union knew the prices for different vodka volumes by heart. The handy a quarter-litre bottle, with the benefit of fitting in the inner pocket of a jacket, was just a touch excessive for one person and not enough for two. The most popular half-litre bottle for about three rubles was perfect volume-wise for three people and easy to split the cost by collecting a ruble from each one. Vodka, a universally preferred currency for illegal transactions, changed hands for favours. But for a doctor or a teacher, a bottle of cognac looked more appropriate.

Like most Russians, I also drank, but not into numbing unconsciousness. I found a relief valve in talking and arguing with my trusted friends. I also had a trusted fellow teacher, Mikhail, with whom I discussed everything freely. And in the early 80s, I was fortunate to have a bright student with whom I also discussed openly what's going on in the country. He also listened to the "enemy voices." Talk about double talk. During the political hour, I lectured my students about how great our country is and how smart are our party leaders are, and after, I had a different discussion with the smart student.

A glimmer of something to look forward to appeared at a time of total hopelessness. My Soviet misfortunes turned out to be my fortunes; for once I got lucky as Jew. Being Jewish meant that I, at last, had a better chance of emigrating than other ethnicities—essentially the only group eligible for exit visas. Most other inmates of the state were not so fortunate. Some even tried to bribe their way into changing their nationality to Jew. As the famous joke went, "A Jew is not a nationality; a Jew is a mode of transportation." Marrying a Jew could transport a non-Jew out of the country when the spouse got permission to leave. That prompted one of my students to ask me why we have the fifth line in on our passports. I never asked myself this question and was intrigued by it. I did some research.

The regime legalized the concept of 'nationality' in the 1920s when all Soviet citizens were required to have a passport. When I reached sixteen, the state issued an internal passport for me. Since no such thing as international travel for ordinary citizens existed, we didn't need another kind of passport. This passport played the role of an ID, like a driver's license in the US. It contained the last name, the first name, the patronymic, the date of birth, and the notorious 'fifth line' that announced one's 'nationality': Russian, or Ukrainian, or Armenian, or Greek, or Jew. There were a lot of nationalities in the Soviet empire, more than one hundred. You could be a citizen of Ukraine, for instance, but if ethnically you were an Armenian, that was your 'nationality'. That meant that I did not have a legal right to call myself Russian or Ukrainian. Even though I was born and lived my whole life in Ukraine, I had never called myself Ukrainian. I couldn't even if I wanted to, though it would have made my life easier. I was a Jew. For laughs, we called it an *invalid* (cripple) of the fifth line.

If the Soviets just eliminated the fifth line of the internal passports, they could have assimilated hundreds of thousands of Jews who had no reason other than that line to think of themselves as Jews. An ethnicity dies when their language and culture die. The fifth lane may have been the most effective factor in maintaining our Jewish identity. If not for the fifth line, within a generation or two, the total assimilation, or spiritual genocide of Soviet Jews, would have been completed. Ironically, what kept me apart from the local population, unlike my ancestors, was not my religion or language—the regime deprived me of both—but my birth certificate and the fifth line in my passport that stated my 'nationality' as Jew and reminded me and everyone else who I was.

The fifth line, when combined with a Jewish-sounding name and sturdy nose, was the equivalent of a yellow star. So, even if my last name Grinshpun, my first name Yakov, and my patronymic Isaakovich, which meant son of Isaac, didn't reveal my nationality (and mine screamed Jew), there would be no doubt about it when filling out paperwork. I was the incontrovertible product of shtetl breeding. Because of that, my post-World War II generation of Jews felt ashamed of their Jewish names. My neighbour Sara became Sima, my friend Abram became Aleksandr, and the shtetl butcher Moyshe became Mikhail. My half-brother's name, whom I knew as Mika, was, during the war, changed to Maxim. I don't know what his legal name was before. There was a joke about a physicist who defended a dissertation based on the work of 'great physicist Odnokamushkin'. Odnokamushkin sounded Russian enough, except for being a literal translation of Einstein.

The student who asked the question was Russian, but her last name was very Jewish—Shpigelman. She had a difficult time fitting in. 'Jew' would be the word on the fifth line under the 'nationality' in passports, save when one parent was not Jewish and a child adopted the non-Jewish parent's nationality. In this case, people or, more likely, their parents could choose the last name and nationality of one of the parents. As a rule, people in mixed marriages chose the non-Jewish 'nationality' and the non-Jewish-sounded last name. And who knows how many Jewish Fathers swallowed their masculine pride to give their children the Russian-sounding names of their wives. Being and sounding non-Jewish was essential for success. Many Jews dreamed to hide behind a narrow curtain of non-Jewish-sounding names, any name—Russian, Ukrainian, Armenian. Life would be a great deal easier for an Ivanov than for a Weinstein. We knew early on in life that names ending with 'ov' were Russian and names ending with 'stein' were Jewish. By the way, the great chess champion Gary Kasparov was born Garry Weinstein. Because of the anti-Semitic prejudice, his coaches, after his father died in a car accident, suggested a change in name to his mother's maiden name Kasparov since Weinstein could inhibit his chess career. He has taken on his mother's last name that had a Russian flavour to it. My cousin's wife's father had his nationality changed from Jew to Russian in the chaos of World War II. Because of that, he had a position in the judicial system and his daughter could enter a medical school. My father-in-law, also during World War II, changed his name from Gershman to Gershmanov, which sounded more Russian. The identity of Jews was being delineated for us by our enemies. We'd paid our dues to our 'nationality'. The state and our fellow citizens made sure of that. Subtle and not-so-subtle discrimination against Jews was frustrating and depressing.

By the early 1970s, the relentless pressure from the West, especially from the United States and its Jewish constituency, forced the Kremlin to change the policy of denials and allow Jews, in limited numbers, to immigrate to Israel, officially for 'family reunification'. Jews had become an exchange currency in the battles of the cold war. The Soviet government, seeking détente with the West and the economic benefit of most-favoured-nation status, allowed a limited number of Jews to leave for Israel. However, numerous hurdles designed to minimize or stem the flow of Jews out of the country were introduced. The authorities were afraid that the Jewish emigration movement would spread to other ethnic minorities. The regime claimed it permitted emigration for the humanitarian reasons of family reunification, with the Jewish State the only destination. A few Jews got out of the country after receiving invitations from relatives in Israel. Because there were no direct flights to Israel, a few on the way to Israel 'dropped out' in Vienna and applied to come to the United States as political refugees.

In 1974, the U.S. Congress passed an amendment to the law granting the Soviet Union the most-favoured-nation status which tied the aid to the Soviet Union to let Soviet Jews leave the country. The Soviet regime reacted defensively, slipping into full-blown repression and cutting down sharply on Jewish emigration. Exit visa requests were denied and many Jews who had already applied for them lost their jobs, creating the category of refuseniks—people refused the right to leave the country. But the outflow did not stop entirely. After the 1975 Helsinki Accord signed by European countries and the U.S., Canada, and the Soviet Union and economic pressure from the United States, more Jews left the country. Officially, no one was supposed to want to leave the Soviet 'paradise', otherwise how to grandstand to the world about the quality of life of the Soviet people if they wanted to leave. The Soviet authorities, needing economic help from the West and courting the world before the 1980 Olympics in Moscow, loosened restrictions to Jewish emigration in the late 1970s.

Because the authorities would allow Jews to immigrate to Israel only for family reunification reasons, this created a problem. Soviet Jews had few relatives in Israel. Sadly, or as later it turned out, fortunately, I had relatives abroad, but not in Israel. Israel had the task of locating needed relatives. The solution—create fictitious relatives. To do this Israelis needed basic demographics, such as names, birthdays, birthplaces, addresses, etc. from people looking for 'reunification'. The Soviet authorities quickly realised that and at once clamped down on all outgoing communication with Israel. Phone lines and the mail were heavily monitored. The few people permitted to leave the country were searching for any kind of documentation and, therefore, were afraid to smuggle the necessary information. People counterbalanced it by keeping the information encrypted and concealed.

Until the mid-seventieth, the stream of Jews leaving the country still a trickle, I had given little thought to emigration. By 1977 reality was gaining ground. As more people applied for exit visas and Jews left the country in considerable numbers thanks to efforts by Soviet refuseniks and American advocates, I became restless. Two kinds of forces played the role, desire to get out and fear. Fear manifested itself in two ways. If Jews applied for permission to emigrate, no certainty the authority would grant it. If they refused our exit visa, it would result in losing our jobs. We had no other skills. How would we feed ourselves? Refusniks were excluded from most jobs, even many of those otherwise available to Jews. Rejection could mean years of penury and official harassment. The other fear was of losing the opportunity to escape. The time marked by the massive emigration of Jews was a time of bewilderment, fear, and hope. By 1978 the fear of missing a chance at freedom became stronger than the fear of consequences and I began to actively consider emigration.

Chapter 21

The first step was to talk to Mila.

"Mila," I said. "I know you told me a decade ago not to even talk about emigration. I respected your wishes. But I couldn't stop thinking. Now the situation has changed, and we need to talk."

She tilted her head and looked at me with interest. *It's a good sign.* I plunged ahead.

"Years passed, a lot of things changed, but the political system remained the same, as did the 'Jew' on the fifth line in our passports and anti-Semitism that goes with it." I stopped to gather my thoughts.

"There is no hope it will change here for the better for us. If not about our lives, think about Rika. I don't see a future for her here." I looked at her again. Something in her eyes told me she was receptive to the conversation.

"Can we talk now?"

"Yes, but don't talk to Rika about that." Besides the sadness in her eyes, I saw expectation. "I'm afraid," she continued. "We have an established life here. And what about my parents? What about our friends?"

We found ourselves between a rock and a hard place: hating the State that hates us and loving the people and places of our youth.

"I understand. It's such a responsibility. I'm not sure that with my rudimentary English I could find a job as a teacher abroad. They say we would have to eat a lot of 'crap' until it would become better. I am afraid for us it would be worse because of our professions."

"That's what I'm talking about. My degree in the German language wouldn't be of help either."

We sat for a while, looking at each other.

"You know, we don't have to decide right now. Let me take several preliminary steps. Okay?"

This evening, not explicitly, we made a difficult and potentially hazardous decision to leave our home, family, and friends and start a new life. After a few months of brooding, we decided to leave the country for good—a difficult and dangerous decision. We decided to leave not because we no longer wanted to live here but because we no longer were able to. Living under the brutal regime became more and more difficult. When lines are drawn, we all choose sides. Dive in and be scared later.

It takes a lot of courage to fight an oppressive regime; you have to be a hero. It is even scarier for an ordinary person to venture into the unknown. The unknown is frightening. In addition to the fear of authorities, there were pitfalls of the process and the prospect of being refused the exit visa. In the end, by luck or by draw, we would become either refuseniks or refugees. It was a matter of major consequence attempting to leave the country.

The next day we went to our friends Ilya and Dina. They had experience with the matter, an unfortunate one. They, together with Dina's parents and two brothers, went through the whole process. Everyone had permission to leave but Ilya and Dina. The reason stated, he served in the army and knew state secrets. The family emigrated and they were left behind as refuseniks. Both were fired from their jobs—he as a computer programmer and she as a musician.

"Guys," I said, "walk us through the process."

"So, you decided to leave?" Ilya looked at us.

"Before making the final decision we want to find out what steps to take to be prepared." I looked at Mila. She nodded.

"Yes, it's a difficult decision," Dina said. "Just look at us. But above the weight of making the decision and risking to be refused with all the consequences to follow there's something else."

"There's always something else," Mila said, "Well, let's hear it. What is it?"

"The authorities put a lot of constraints to discourage even thinking about leaving."

These restrictions didn't cause a lot of headaches for us. They were unfortunate, but not personal. But the growing anti-Semitism, economic difficulties, and educational and occupational quotas forced even successful and somewhat assimilated Jews to question what would become of their children if they remained in the country.

"That's why we came here, to learn what to be prepared for," I said.

"First you would need money, a lot." Ilya took over. "They would deprive you of citizenship and charge 700 rubles per person for that. Then they impose an educational tax on people with a college degree because, as they argued, higher education in the Soviet Union was free. You would have to compensate the state for the amount spent on your education."

"We would sell our coop and all our belongings, so I think it won't be a problem. And we will start saving," I said.

"They also demanded parents' permission for children to leave the country on the pretence that parents may later in life need their support. Are your parents also leaving?" Ilya looked at Mila.

"I think it won't be a problem," she said.

"And finally," Ilya continued. "They demand people ask for permission to leave from employers, which in most times would result in being fired and oftentimes in denunciation at public meetings. And I hope the authorities can't connect you to any state secrets, it's a hundred percent refusal of the exit visa."

At that moment, I recalled what happened to a teacher of the Ukrainian language at my school who applied for an exit visa to Israel. The termination followed immediately. Because the authorities required a kharacteristika (a letter of character) from the last place of employment, she had to come to a meeting where we discussed and voted for the letter—the voting a mere formality. We all raised our hands when the Party organizer read a prepared letter. It was brutal. Denounced as a traitor and an enemy of the people, the teacher stood there, shoulders slump, the head bent. Some people did it sincerely, others because they had to if they wanted to work as teachers. Luckily, the principal didn't call me to speak. The truth sat at the back of my throat, choking me for not letting it out. Oh, how I longed for a fight. But I learned that discretion is the best part of valour. Over time, I had already developed an intense gag reflex. I felt uncomfortable and couldn't even imagine how the former teacher felt. There were anecdotes of people leaving such meetings with a heart attack.

Just as suddenly as I flashed back, I returned to the present.

"So, what should we do first?" I said.

"The first step, you have to receive a vyzov (summon) from relatives in Israel," he said, holding up his hand to forestall my protest. "Yeah, yeah, I know that you don't have any."

I looked with interest at him, waiting for him to continue. "Find a way to send your information abroad, and Jewish organizations will find you 'relatives'." He paused. "And begin studying English."

I didn't start learning English, but I found the way. A neighbour of ours, Sana, had permission to leave the country, and we decided to ask her to smuggle our personal information. In Vienna, she would give it to Sokhnut, the Jewish agency, and they would arrange an invitation for a family reunion (with fictitious relatives) in Israel. We would pretend that our reason for leaving is merely familial, and the State would pretend that it believes us. We wrote down our information on a piece of paper and went to see Sana.

"Sana," I said, "would you take this to Vienna?"

"I can't take this piece of paper. If they find it, I'd be in trouble and so would you." She smiled a sad smirk.

We fell silent. She smiled again, this time a superior smile.

"Among the would-be emigrants," she said, "there are a few methods of smuggling the information. One of them is to write information on underpants' elastic."

In Soviet underwear, the elastic band was removable. She opened one of her suitcases and took out a pair of underpants. She removed the band and stretched it to the maximum. My nerves were also stretched to the maximum.

"Write the information down on it."

When we let the band return to its natural length, all we could see was a blue stripe. She put the band back into its place. We knew that we couldn't outsmart the KGB and just hoped that the Customs officers wouldn't have the capacity to check every pair of underpants.

We were not at all sure that we would get an invitation, so we tried a few more times with other people willing to deliver our information to the Jewish organizations. And we did receive an invitation, even two. A funny, as I think of it now, thing happened with the first invitation. I worked at school on the first shift. My middle-grade daughter attended the second shift. One day she came to my classroom during the last period and excitedly said, "Look what a strange letter we received."

I quickly grabbed the oversized letter in the colours of the Israeli flag before my students could see it. The situation could end in disaster for me. The day I received the summon, I didn't have anything on my mind other than getting the hell away from this country, and quick.

To receive a *vyzov* (summon) gave no guarantee of leaving, but was a necessary first step. Next, we had to collect the necessary signatures that the authority demanded: from employers, building superintendents, and parents just to name a few. We started with the easiest one, a letter signed by my parents-in-law stating that they didn't object to us leaving the country. According to the emigration procedure, parents had to release children before the State did. Ostensibly, the reason was financial, to prevent prodigal children from abandoning their parents, in reality, to put more obstacles and pressure on the applicants. Unexpectedly, this step created a problem for us. My father-in-law refused to sign the letter. I kind of understood where he came from. As a member of the Communist Party, he had a good job he was afraid of losing it. As a veteran of the Great Patriotic War, he had other benefits—a phone, a special food store, skipping a line. He paid with silence for those privileges. But I couldn't understand and forgive his selfishness in deciding our fate for us. I tried to reason with him, but the reason has a toothless mouth. My mother-in-law, a smart and strong woman, kind of understood where we are coming from but she said: "I don't want to live through another evacuation." She referred to her experiences of fleeing Odessa before the Nazi occupation and the difficult three years in Siberia. "I don't want to relive those experiences. It's a feeling I only wish on my worst enemy." I wasn't sure if it was a hundred percent genuine, or she just supported her husband, but it was hard to watch. I would spare her if I could. Mad and disappointed, I looked at their heartbroken faces. The price of broken hearts you paid for rescuing your family. "May the day never come when you feel the pain I feel now," she added with tears in her eyes.

While we were trying to persuade him to change his mind, the authorities slammed shut the door to Jewish emigration. When the Soviet Union invaded Afghanistan in 1979, Jimmy Carter imposed a wheat embargo and boycotted the 1980 Moscow summer Olympics. The Soviet Union had nothing to gain from getting their Jews to go. The authorities retaliated by drastically reducing Jewish emigration. For every one permitted to leave nine would be refused and sentenced to a life as traitors—unemployable and subjects to KGB harassment. Emigration in the Soviet Union was a one-way street; leaving or trying to leave equated to betrayal. The ruling body of the country, the Politburo, consisted mostly of old, sick, and typically poorly-educated people. Like old joints, they were inflexible. The joke, "How the next Congress of the Communist Party would start?" The answer, "With words 'wheel in the Politburo'." With those old people staying in line to be the next 'tsar', the change seemed unlikely in the foreseeable future.

We missed the train of emigration and got stuck in the Soviet Union. Did it mean to happen?

We shouldn't have ruminated for so long and should have starting work on parents earlier. We should've anticipated that the emigration trapdoor might close shut. Should've. There's an Odessa expression "wise as my Sara afterward." A few years later, we figured out that 1979 was the peak year for Jewish emigration that dwindled to a paltry number after that. Even though the release of Soviet Jews was the condition for receiving the status of the "most-favoured-nation," the authorities decided to stop the exodus of Jews from the socialist paradise. Change in our lot seemed unachievable. The 1970s ended with a lost opportunity. For ten years, emigration remained our obsession. From the late 1970s to after the mid-1980s, when the Soviet Union occupied Afghanistan and President Reagan was getting tough on what he called the "evil empire," emigration from the country slowed to a trickle.

For years, every time I thought of the lost opportunity to leave the country, I found myself tormented, angry, and eaten up inside. As the years grew into a decade, so did my longing for a different life. I could think of nothing but escaping the Soviet Union. It seemed we were stuck here permanently. But only death is permanent.

Chapter 22

On November 10, 1982, I arrived at school worrying. In place of regular programming, radio and television broadcast sad classical music. *What's going on? There would be changes, and they may be good or, most likely, bad.* I sat quietly in the small windowless room adjacent to my physics classroom. *Would they allow, whatever happened, Jewish emigration?* If I had a daisy, I would tear off the petals—allow, allow not—hoping that the last one would be an allow.

The door opened and my fellow teacher and trusted friend Mikhail, with a cigarette in hand, entered the room. His pocket as usually bulged with a pack of Sever—a Russian style cigarette. He immediately lit up the unfiltered cigarette and took a long draw. He exhaled, and his bald head with spectacles propped on it was shrouded by cigarette smoke. Baldness was not the main thing that we had in common. We were kindred spirits and saw the situation in the country not as the Party wanted us to see. He was not only the right stuff, but he had the right stuff—smart, educated, and quick-witted. Trusting each other, we discussed problems honestly without fear of being reported to the school's Party organizer. He was fifteen years older and had a big influence on me. One maxim of his I still try to follow: *95% of all problems solve themselves. The remaining 5% don't have a solution; nothing to worry about.*

"It's a good time if you like classical music," he said.

"Yeah, I listened till late and this morning."

"The last time they played this long was if I remember right when Stalin died." He lowered his voice, "Someone important kicked the bucket."

"Yeah. Do you think it's Brezhnev?" I touched my chin. "Despite what you taught me, I am worried." I fell silent. "I am about forty years old, give or take, not a dumb kid anymore, but not yet an old man either. And I'm not getting any younger. And Brezhnev is not getting any older. I've been thinking it's not too late to start a new life somewhere." Now, he fell silent.

"What could happen? Would it help me? Could I leave?" I fired a string of questions.

"You're asking the wrong questions."

"What're the right questions?"

"I don't know."

"Who will be our new boss?"

"I don't know. But if it would be Andropov, forget about leaving."

The habitual caution, humiliating fear, and all-pervasive insecurity made him pause and look over his shoulder even though we were alone. He tossed his smoke into a garbage can and lit another.

"Looks like it will be another septuagenarian." After a pause, he said, "His life may have ended, but I doubt yours would change." I looked at him. "Of course, there will be changes, but I guess the next boss wouldn't allow Jewish emigration. Don't count on it."

I would never escape.

"So, I will be stuck here forever?" I held back tears. The bell rang, and we went to our respective classes.

Around eleven the principal gathered the whole school in a wide recreational corridor, a row of doors on one side, and a row of windows on another. The gloom of the fall sky pouring through a window after a window didn't improve my mood. After we tried to quiet the students, the principal came forward. She wore no makeup and a black dress trailing from her fleshy shoulders, stiff as a clothes mannequin. Her face matched the sky. Silence followed. The students were afraid of her as well as the teachers.

"The Central Committee of the Party," she scanned the crowd with unusually scared eyes, "with great sorrow announced the passing of General Secretary comrade Brezhnev."

There was an audible gasp as hundreds of people inhaled in unison. It felt as if the air left the room. She went with the usual dog and pony show, talking of prosperity under him. Prosperity? I thought about how much effort I had to exert to find food in stores. And I couldn't afford the Privoz market prices. The daily drama of putting a meal on the table trumped most other concerns of daily life. Food expenses were a disproportionally large part of one's monthly salary. A family was well-to-do if they had ten to fifteen percent of their salary left for other than food expenses. Food defined how the overwhelming majority of Soviet people endured the present and imagined the future. Paradoxically, empty store shelves often meant full pantries and stuffed fridges. The only thing that mattered was nutritional content; the more calories, the better. Food being bad for your health? Forget about this. Sugar was good, fat even better, and bread altogether sacred.

I doubt many believed the principal, but Brezhnev's eighteen-year-long reign was a period not dominated by terrors, cataclysms, and conflicts—a paradise in contrast to previous reigns. I tried to read her facial expression but couldn't decide if it were real sorrow or apprehension of what the future would bring or both. I also was apprehensive, but unlike her, under the ashes of reality, the sparks of hope that they will again open the door to Jewish emigration showed signs of life.

"Eighteen is a lucky number for Jews," Mikhail said after the meeting when we were alone.

"I know, although I don't know why."

"It means life." Mikhail caught the time when Jewish education was allowed in the country.

"Well, that's where I'm stuck in life?"

"I suppose. That's life."

"Why don't you give me a cigarette." My lips quivered.

"You're near tears, aren't you?" After a pause. "With a bit of luck, eighteen means a better life."

Brezhnev opened, under American pressure, the door for Jewish emigration in the mid-70s. That's when we, after contemplating for a couple of years, made an unsuccessful attempt to emigrate and missed the train trying to persuade my in-laws to sign an essential paper. My father-in-law was smart but, to mildly say, not at all courageous. His fear of losing his good job and his Party membership with privileges that went with it was stronger than his parental instincts. This time, instead of persuasion, I was ready to confront him should the possibility of getting out come about.

The next two days both channels of Soviet TV were filled with displaying how Soviet people said goodbye to dear comrade Brezhnev and with his televised funeral. Yes, we had only two channels. There was a joke. If you change the channels beyond the two official ones, the much-feared chairman of the KGB Andropov would appear on the screen pointing a finger at you and asking: "What else are you looking for?"

On the day of the funeral, we went to the in-laws to watch the procession. They had a large TV and a big room that could accommodate the whole family. The funeral procession, I would say now, was worthy of an Oscar. The Red Square was full of wreaths from each of the Soviet Union republics, autonomous republics, regions, and ministries. There were hundreds of Brezhnev's portraits in military and civilian dresses, with over two hundred medals he liked to be rewarded with for different occasions, even the invented ones.

As we watched the funeral, my father-in-law asked: "What would happen if a crocodile swallowed Brezhnev?" Everyone looked at him anticipating a nice *anekdot*. "It would shit medals for a week." We all laughed. He grinned. "Would you permit us to leave if the new leadership opens the door?" I waited for him to respond. He did not say anything, so I went on. "Or would you again decide our fate for us?"

As I was studying his reaction, the grin slid off his face as fast as the sandcastle is erased by the incoming wave.

"We will see." He crossed his arms. His lips pressed together in a thin line of upset.

"What does that mean? Could you be more specific, please?" I shook my head.

There was such a long pause that I wondered whether he was ever going to speak.

"It means we'll see." He was struggling for an answer. "It depends on who will give the first speech." His expression was half shame and half anger.

I looked at Mila. Her narrowed eyes focused on him, but she said nothing. So, did her sister.

The former KGB chief Yuriy Andropov delivered the first speech. This was the hint. Sure enough, the next day at the plenum meeting of the Party's Central Committee he was elected to the highest office in the land. My heart sank at the news. Having a KGB man at the helm of the country meant doom for our hope to leave the country. The Soviet Union hated its Jews but needed us to survive

119

in the geopolitical struggle. Because of the dire economic situation, Andropov couldn't afford any brain drain. Jews still constituted, despite quotas at universities and research institutes, the most elite class of technocrats who kept the country on pace with the United States. He hoped that if he stopped even the low level of emigration that existed, Jews might just accept their fate and abandon the dream of leaving. Emigration in 1983 had reached a record low of thirteen hundred. It might as well have been zero to the many of us who couldn't leave. Andropov had a hard heart and implemented draconian changes to put the country on the right track. One of the most ridiculous was an order for the militia to go to the cinemas, during the day, and inquire why people are not at work. But nothing is permanent except death. Even though Andropov had a hard heart, his kidneys were weak. In a few months, he ruled from the hospital bed connected to a dialysis machine. Everything that was happening in the Soviet Union was food for an *anekdot.*

Why Brezhnev went abroad and Andropov didn't?
Because Brezhnev ran on batteries and Andropov needed an outlet. (A reference to Brezhnev's pacemaker and Andropov's dialysis machine.)

After thirteen months of his rule, we had another funeral. Not all funerals are sad. Again, the whole school was gathered for a meeting. It was not as solemn as the first one, but not yet ridiculous. After another gathering of the whole school, Mikhail and I went to the physics lab. He lit up a cigarette.

"Who do you think will be the next one?" I said.

"It looks like Chernenko is next in line."

"Another septuagenarian?" I said in disbelief. "It will be foolish."

Sure enough, an old sick man, Chernenko, was elected. There was a joke: *"Without regaining consciousness, Comrade Chernenko has been elected to the post of General Secretary."* Soon another funeral, another meeting at the school; if the first meeting was rather tragic, the last one was comic.

Chapter 23

The physical and mental deterioration of the leadership was impossible to ignore. With the death of three consecutive General Secretaries of the Communist party in almost as many years—a fantastic stroke of good fortune, sorry to say this—a hope that things might change emerged. Now, electing another septuagenarian to lead the country would be ridiculous. So, the 54-year-old Mikhail Gorbachev, the little-known agricultural secretary of the Central Committee with functioning organs, became the sixth and the last, as it turned out, General Secretary.

Brezhnev, Andropov, and Chernenko chat in heaven (or in hell): "So, who supports Gorbachev these days?"

"Nobody, it seems. I'm as surprised as you. It looks as if he's able to walk on his own."

He appeared more modern and pragmatic and certainly more educated than his predecessors. He travelled around the country and talked about change. The first change was he travelled and appeared in public with his wife. Wives of top leaders were never seen. In a while, we started hearing talks about Glasnost and Perestroika (openness and restructuring). Clouds were gathering over the entire country. Gorbachev opened the windows, and a fierce gale of change blew through the system. Glasnost meant more than just the freedom to curse the government in the streets rather than in one's kitchen with the water running and the radio blaring. We started to see real changes that led in time to the demise of the Union. Forbidden books such as Boris Pasternak's *Doctor Zhivago* trickled into print. To everyone's amazement, even Solzhenitsyn's works were authorized for publication. Gone were the days of mandatory subscriptions to *Pravda* and the likes. Limits on magazine subscriptions were lifted. People were hungrier for the food for the soul than they were for actual food. I could not believe that the change was genuine and just hoped there wouldn't be a sudden turn back.

As the 'evil empire' started slowly to disintegrate, traveling to Western countries and even leaving the country permanently became less difficult. This opened the door for people to spread information, either personally or through letters, about real life in the West. Even the Soviet elite class saw that the benefits the regime affords them are not worth supporting the communist rule. This eventually destroyed the communist regime and the country as well.

In 1987, virtually everyone, who had been waiting for years as refuseniks, was allowed to leave the country. That's when our friends Ilya and Dina were granted an exit visa to the United States after being refuseniks for close to a decade. We anxiously waited for feedback from them. We waited for a while. When we finally received news from them, it didn't sound optimistic despite that they had their family who lived for ten years in the United States. They wrote that people like my cousin Vladimir, a computer programmer, and his wife Zoya, a dentist, should immigrate to the United States and people like me, a teacher, and Mila, with a degree in the German language, should not. People like me and Mila, in their opinion, wouldn't be able to find a decent job.

But the future was uncertain. Glasnost also had unleashed certain demons. Anti-Semitic groups like Pamyat' (Memory) blamed the Jews for the breakdown of their society. They were calling for blood. Then, an ethnic conflict between two Soviet republics, Armenia and Azerbaijan, happened. It sent a chill down my spine. *Would the pogroms reemerge?*

"That's what you waited for?" I asked my father-in-law. He said nothing. The Soviet Union, marked throughout its tumultuous history by great achievements and terrible suffering, was in a long decline. Where the decline would lead no one knew. It was safer to watch the results from outside. We were determined to get out if not for our sake then for our daughter's.

By 1988, ten years after our first aborted attempt, the circumstances changed and we decided to try again to get out. Still, the authorities permitted them to leave the country only for family reunification. I went without delay to Moscow to renew the expired summon from the fictitious relatives in Israel. The Soviet Union terminated diplomatic relations with Israel after the disastrous (for the Soviet Union) Six-Day War of 1967. Since the war, Israeli interest in the Soviet Union was represented by the Netherlands. I spent the next few days standing in line at the Dutch embassy with excited and nervous Soviet Jews—from Odessa to Omsk and every place between.

"Yakov Isaakovich," I heard out of the blue. Turning around, I saw one of my students.

"What are you doing here?" It was all I could come with.

"Same as you," he answered.

Worrying, I said, "You know that you can't tell at school you saw me here."

Despite liberalization, my choice to emigrate was a gamble. Everything depended on the government issuing us exit visas. Failure would cost us our jobs and the ability to support ourselves. Although certain restrictions were removed, such as automatic firing and the ban to take any document but the visa out of the country, the authorities forgot to announce that to the general public. We didn't need the parents' permission any longer, we were free to take our papers with us, and it wasn't automatic firing from your job. Local powers knew of the changes but not us. That it was easier to leave didn't mean it was easy. The Soviet Union was already teetering but still standing.

Soviet Jews became free to stay or leave, embrace their Jewishness or assimilate. The choice was theirs to make. In light of Gorbachev's liberalization, the United States redefined the refugee status for Soviet Jews. Now, they had to prove a 'well-founded fear of persecution' to come to America as refugees. Starting October 1, 1989, the United States would no longer process Soviet Jews in Rome. Visas would be issued in Moscow, and preference would be given to people who had close family members already in the United States. They set a quota for Soviet Jews who can come to the country on the family reunification process. We would barely could do it just in time.

To get into the United States I needed a guarantor—a person who would guarantee that they would not allow the new immigrants to accept public assistance. The problem was that I didn't know anyone in America who could do it for me. For the most part, immigrants of post-1987 needed families or friends to provide temporary housing and food, and sign guarantees. With a guarantor, I was assured access to the United States. I desperately tried to solve the problem, to no avail. Then, I recalled that my father told me his oldest sister immigrated to America, but I knew nothing about the family. That's where the two letters my father received from his sisters in Mexico and Argentina decades earlier could help. He passed away twenty years ago, but my sister kept his papers. Thank God. Without delay, I went to the closest phone booth and called her.

"Riva," I said, "do you remember papa received letters from his sisters abroad?"

"No, I don't," she said after a pause.

"How can't you remember? I do, and I was only a child then."

"I lived in another city already, and you were still at home."

"Okay, it doesn't matter. Just look for them. I'll call you in an hour." I didn't have a phone, and she was lucky to have one.

Exactly in an hour, I called her again and gasped when she said she found the letters. The same evening, I boarded an overnight train to retrieve them.

Among the papers at the bottom of the box with father's staff, I found the two letters. The letters were yellowed and brittle and carried a scent of a distant past. But to me, they were more valuable than gold. The letters were in Yiddish with its Hebrew alphabet. I couldn't read them. The addresses were in the Latin alphabet, and that was all I needed. With the help of a dictionary, I wrote two simple letters having little hope for a response. A month later I received a letter from my cousin in Argentina who I didn't even know existed. I quickly wrote a second letter asking if they knew about our relatives in the United State. I was gasping for air when the next letter had the address of my American cousin in Margate, Florida. I wrote to him and after a week began to check the mailbox a few times every day, including weekends. It took a while, but at last, I got the answer. I grabbed the letter and sprinted to the fifth floor without opening it. No elevators, of course.

"Look what I have," I shouted. Mila from the kitchen and Rika from the room materialized in the tiny foyer.

"Open it," they said in one voice.

It took me a while because I didn't want to damage the envelope. Evelyn, my cousin's Alan wife, wrote how excited they were to hear from the family. They were not sure if we survived the Holocaust. The problem of a guarantor was gone. I didn't think my cousin would refuse to be my guarantor. Right away I wrote a response. I didn't care about grammar as long as they would understand what I need.

A few weeks passed until I received an answer. Again, it was Evelyn who wrote that she and Alan discussed the guarantor problem. "The Jewish Federation of Broward County had no experience in handling refugees," she wrote. Didn't know what Broward and what County means and didn't care. My heart firmly lodged in my throat. The next sentence pushed it back. "Alan's sister in New York is going to be your guarantor because in New York the Jewish organizations know how to handle immigrants."

That's when I started on the necessary steps in earnest. First, we talked to parents.

"There is a chance for us to leave the country," I said. They said nothing. It was on me to continue. "Last time, you decided our fate for us. Now, I won't allow you to do it to us again." I Looked at Mila. She looked at no one. "We are leaving, and don't stop us again."

The climate in the country changed, and, I thought, my father-in-law stopped worrying about what would happen to him if he signed the letter not objecting to our decision to emigrate. This time, I thought, they understood they were wrong the first time. Problem solved. Who knew that permission from parents was not necessary by now?

Second, I'd got myself on the list of would-be emigrants that maintained orderly submission of the application to OVIR for exit visas. The wait was more than a month. I had to check every weekend in a park in the city centre to remain on the list.

One more unpleasant task remained. I had to notify my principal, knowing I would be fired and chastised. Images of the teacher chastised ten years earlier by colleagues made my heart quicken. I worked with the principal for eighteen years and felt uncomfortable putting her in a difficult situation. One day, looking on my raised hand for a while, I knocked at her door. When I heard, "Come in," I slipped into her office and stood silent for a few seconds. She looked at me.

"Lidia Andreevna," I coughed against my hand. "I have bad news for you."

She kept her eyes on me, and I held my breath, "I'm planning to emigrate."

"But now it's not a betrayal." Her face relaxed, even a hint of a smile appeared.

Wide-eyed I looked at her. I heard what she said, and I didn't. My mind just couldn't comprehend that it would be so simple. Who knew that now emigration was not a betrayal? She knew, but I didn't. We discussed something but nothing about me being fired. On my way out, I closed the door quietly. A long exhale left my lungs.

Under the communist regime, real estate assets such as apartments, by and large, belonged to the state. As an emigrant, I had to cede my apartment and bring proof of that before I received the exit visa. After that, we had to clear the apartment. Whatever we accumulated during our Soviet life, we sold or gave to friends and relatives. The most valued thing, the wall unit imported from Czechoslovakia we gave to the parents. I thought about how for about a year I had to go to the furniture store every week to assure that I am on the waiting list for the unit. I remembered how proud I was when I finally get the unit into my apartment.

When we emptied the apartment, we stood there and looked at each other. Mila went to the window and began caressing the windowsill and storage I build under it. She was crying.

"Do you remember when you put it together? I was so proud of you."

I came up to her and hugged her. She put her head on my shoulder. "You spent so much energy and money using every trick to make the shattered apartment liveable." She sobbed. "And now we have to give it back for nothing."

"With any luck, we would have something better." I felt my eyes beginning to moist.

After the fall of the Soviet Union, a lot of laws were cancelled. When my in-laws fled independent Ukraine in 1993, they kept their assets and also their citizenship. The citizenship was of no use, but they, unlike us, came to America with some money they made selling their privatized apartment. My father-in-law benefitted again.

We locked the door for the last time, and I took the keys to the housing authorities. They gave me a piece of paper proving that I surrendered the apartment, and I brought it to OVIR to have the final stamp on the exit papers. We paid seven hundred rubbles per person for them to strip us of our citizenship and surrendered our hammer and circle red Soviet passports with the hated fifth line, knowing we wouldn't be able to come back. As far as I was concerned, I didn't need to come back. I was, if lucky, done with the Soviet Union. It was my last official deal with the hated state.

From now on, until we would leave the country, our proofs of identities were Soviet-issued exit visas with black-and-white frenzied photos. For a few years, we would be passport-less.

Chapter 24

On July 6, 1989, we packed our Soviet lives in suitcases and boarded a train to Moscow. All our friends and relatives came to see us off. As it became customary, I had a couple of bottles of vodka and disposal cups and we drank together for the last time at the platform of the Odessa train station. People who planned to leave the country toasted: "See you soon in America, God willing." People who didn't have such plans: "Hope you would come to visit us." In the end, all of them left the Soviet Union or its remnants and were scattered all over the world.

After America restricted immigration from the former Soviet Union only to close relatives, Israel became the main destination for Soviet Jews who wanted to get out. Close to a million Jews escaped to Israel. Today, Israel can look at its transformation into a start-up nation and be thankful for this infusion of intellectual power; seventy percent of new immigrants had college degrees.

The few days in Moscow before we left for Vienna to start our immigrant saga, we spent mostly on shopping. When we, God willing, arrive in the United States, we would be, virtually, penniless. People advised us to buy things we would need after arrival. They told me to buy five costumes because when I would find a job, I would need to wear a different suit every working day. This was the main thing. The others were a few pairs of glasses, shaving necessities, and a few cartons of cigarettes. Only the latter saved me money. It would be better if instead of all this I bought a few more military watches that were in demand in Italy. We were ready to leave the country. After the last dinner with family and friends, we left for the airport. I have a vague recollection of the ride to the airport. I have an indelible memory of what occurred at the airport.

We were at the gate reserved for those who were 'leaving for permanent residency'—a euphemism for people who could escape the country. The area, designed to make even the innocent feel guilty, packed to capacity. Barriers separated those without citizenship from the 'loyal' citizens. Wailing on either side of the barrier, Jews cried goodbye to their relatives with all the emotions they were well known for, saying farewell forever.

We dragged through another barrier to the checking point, carrying the bags of belongings that took years to accumulate. I had to make three trips to bring the six pieces of luggage. A militiaman commanded to put the luggage on the tables and step back behind the barrier. Policemen in the Soviet Union was a dirty word after the Bolshevik revolution; they called them militiamen instead of policemen. I stood helplessly, watching a uniformed Customs officer approaching the tables. *Would we pass the search safely?*

"Is this all your luggage?" The voice and the glance made my stomach feel as if a knot has been tied in it.

"Yes," I said hoping the fluttering in my stomach didn't make its way into my throat. The question made my hands shake, but it didn't crack my voice. It made my heart beat faster, but it didn't bend my knees.

The authorities allowed two pieces of luggage per person. Into each, we had to pack 20 kg of what used to be our Soviet lives. One piece was a large suitcase, the other a gigantic custom-made sack. The Customs officer opened all six of them. After emptying everything, he patted the inside lining of our suitcases suspecting the double bottom like they always suspected us of double life. The officer decided he should have another sadist in uniform to take a further look. The other officer poked around the lining of the sacks, looking for diamonds we may have stashed within. It seemed like the search went forever. With the KGB thoroughness, they went through every item on the table and fingered every seam in our clothes. My heart thumped so hard I thought they can see it through my shirt. I put my hand to the heart as though warding off a heart attack. Next, it sank deeper than to the stomach, and hair prickled on the back of my neck when they opened a bag with my underpants and found our birth certificates and college diplomas wrapped into it. The unsmiling faces of Customs agents made my guts ready to give up my last meal one way or another. I, more than I thought possible, needed a toilet. I looked at Mila and met her troubled eyes.

"I'm afraid," she whispered.

"I hope the worst that could happen we would have to leave the documents with your parents." Hope in such situations was the only thing available to us. One agent, seeing our exchange, raised his head and looked at me. His gaze hit me like a rogue wave. I shivered, and he relished watching me squirm. I tried to keep anger off my face, but I could feel my face getting hot. He smiled seemingly entertained by my misery. The air was heavy with tension.

It had been forbidden to take any official document out of the country save the visas that promised freedom. Our only proofs of identity were Soviet-issued exit visas with black-and-white unsmiling photos. The papers the officer held in his hands would tell our story in more detail than the visas. I was terrified that because of them they could delay our exit. And who knows what may follow. He put everything back and went to the next bag. I couldn't believe my luck. Relief washed over me like a thunderstorm over parched dirt. Who knew that now they allowed taking personal papers with you? They forgot to announce that. Mila took me by my arm. My breaths quickened. I looked at Rika, she didn't get it.

After they paid little attention to the few military watches, linens, nestling 'matryoshka' dolls, and small jars of caviar we hoped to sell in Italy to have a little money for the rainy days in the West. I felt that the lump in my stomach shrunk. Thank God, they didn't search the intimate parts of our bodies. But one of them, with a smile or a sneer or both on his face, came close to Mila and looked her up from head to toe and back and said, "You can't take your diamond earrings."

"They are not diamonds, they are cubic zirconium," Mila said.

"Don't argue." I put my arm around her shoulder. She looked like she needed cheering up. "Give them to him."

"Take them off, we will check."

He took the earrings and disappeared behind a door.

After a long delay, the officer told us that she couldn't take the earrings with her. He handed them back.

"They are my favourite." Mila's lips began moving in a way that told me she was going to cry. It was the last straw for her. I put my arm around her shoulder again and squeezed her tight.

"What do we do with them?" I asked, mute with misery and anger for a moment.

"Leave them with your relatives."

"Why is he so cruel?" Rika asked when the officer left.

"I kind of understand him," I said. "We are leaving the Soviet Union, but he would never leave."

Mila went to the barrier and gave the earrings to her mother who also started to sob. When Mila came back, she said, "I will never see them again." I couldn't figure out she meant earrings or her parents. We kissed goodbye to relatives from a distance, not sure when and if we would see them again. Rika mouthed something to her grandmother, and she began to shake. The Soviet Union endured for about seventy years, and, as far as I could tell in 1989, would for many more years with its draconian policies. We maybe won't see them again. Exiting Customs into the restricted area of International Departures, I turned to take one last glance at the world I was leaving behind. The last image was of my sister-in-law, Gala, smearing a large tear across her cheek as she waved to us.

It was a relief to get out of Customs—the place of dread and humiliation. We exited outside to where they moved our luggage, only to go from the frying pan to the fire. An official weighed our bags and found them twenty kilograms over the limit.

"What are we to do? Do we have to leave a few items here?" Mila looked crestfallen.

My heart began racing. It was the fear that we could miss our plane, a serious problem. I looked around. My worrying expression caught the eye of a young man in uniform, and he approached me.

"Problems?" he said casually.

"Yes. My luggage is twenty kilograms above the limit."

"No problem, five rubbles per kg, and your problem is solved."

I calculated; six pieces of luggage each 20 kg, plus the 20-kg excess weight is 140kg, times 5 rubles per kg equals 700 rubles.

"I don't have 700 rubles."

"You misunderstood me. It's only for the excess weight."

100 rubles were acceptable. I paid; problem solved.

"If you have anything that you don't want the Customs to look through, I can arrange it; just 300 rubles per suitcase."

"Where were you before?" I said.

"You had to explore."

"Who knew?"

My last, although unofficial, act with the Soviet Union was a hundred rubbles bribe. How emblematic. You live with bribes; you leave with bribes.

I looked up. Clouds glided west rolling onto the distant horizon. The farther west, the lighter the clouds became.

I don't remember boarding the plane marked with Aeroflot's winged hammer and sickle, but I have a vivid memory of the flight itself. On my first international flight, I was, most of the time, lost in thoughts, going over my whole life trying to reconstruct my past to find the real reason why I left. When the door closed, I had carried with me on the plane baggage so heavy that thirty years later I'm still trying to unload it. It was, to a large degree, a dark past and, with a bit of luck, a bright future on the horizon.

Take off and ascent; we were flying west, away from hell, and towards paradise. After taking my seat and catching my breath, I looked around. Although it was an international flight, the plane didn't look nice. Either they didn't tell the truth or the situation in the country became such that authorities didn't care anymore about its image abroad. It looked similar to a domestic flight—the smell, trash on the floor, seats that didn't recline. It didn't matter. What did was that soon Russia would be behind, beyond the mountains, beyond the rivers, and beyond the countries.

"We are leaving the Soviet airspace," an announcement over the loudspeaker interrupted my thoughts and quickened my heart. I looked at Mila and Rika. Mila looked sad and Rika smiled. Some passengers clapped. I could feel my eyes started to well up. I closed my eyes. As our plane crossed the border, in no time we switched from emigrants into immigrants. Just like that, a new era began. Left in the rear was the regime that pushed us out. For most on the plane, including my family, it was the first time we crossed the Soviet border.

For the next couple of hours, until we landed, I kept my eyes closed most of the time so my family wouldn't notice I was worried. All through the flight, I thought of many things—the past we left behind, the future ahead, the regime that pushed us out. But deep down the only thing on my mind was: "We would be in a better world soon." The Moscow-Vienna flight lasted only about three hours, but it amounted to a passage from being within the Soviet bloc to being outside, out of reach. The flight to freedom was short in time but enormous in transformation.

Part IV
A Purgatory of Hope

Chapter 25

From my middle seat, I caught a glimpse of the Vienna International Airport and noted the surrounding farms and wooded areas. As the plane circled the field, I almost refused to believe the reality of our escape. Were we in reality free? It wasn't until the wheels screeched on the tarmac that I let out a sigh of relief. We made it. After we deplaned, I stood with my folks among fellow immigrants bewildered, worried, but happy. So seemed most people in the group. My emotions veered between anxiety and anticipation, between excitement and dread, between elation and disbelief. We reached the West and were out of reach of the Soviet regime. I considered pinching myself to be sure it wasn't a dream; this was such a cliché. I touched my forehead instead.

This was the first stop of what became a three-stop endeavour for Soviet Jews—first Vienna, the triage centre for Soviet immigrants, next Italy for most, and, with any luck, America.

I put my shoulders back to appear confident. "We did it!" I looked at the confused faces of Mila and Rika with a huge smile on mine. A sudden joy of accomplishment overcame me. Mila hugged me and with tears in her voice said: "Thank you." She didn't let me go for a while. What was on Rika's mind I couldn't figure out.

"Rika are you happy?"

"I don't know." She shrugged.

It was a lot for a young girl who graduated only a week earlier to process what was happening. Besides, responsibility was mine, not hers. I stared at them. The thought that I had with me what mattered most to me made my worries insignificant for a while.

Landing in Vienna, representatives of different Jewish groups met the immigrants. A small man in his sixties yelled, "Who is going to Israel?" He had grey hair past due for a cut and a few days' worth of stubble on his face. He was dressed in jeans and an un-tucked grey shirt. His Yiddish-accented Russian reminded me of the way people spoke Russian in my shtetl. I thought about the graves left there. A few people raised their hands, but most remained still and silent not looking at the man. He led the Israel-bound people away.

We got out on Israeli visas and now, we were refusing to go there. I understood why people averted their eyes. This moment carried me back to the time we decided that we want to go to America, barely half a year ago. *Why are we not going to Israel?* The last time I asked this question was during dinner the three of us sat down one evening.

Mila just put three bowels of borscht on the table and we picked up the spoons. I put down my spoon and said, "Now, when we decided to get out of the country, we have to decide where we want to go." Mila glanced at our daughter and they both stared at me, spoons still in their hands. Abandoning everything we knew and had and moving half a world away in search of a chance for a better life was the smartest decision we could make, but the decision of where we want to go was still in the making.

"Rika," I said. "You are the main reason we are doing this. Where do you want to go?"

"I don't know, papa. I know I don't want us to go to Israel."

"Why are we not going to Israel?" It surprised me that for the first time she expressed a definite opinion about the whole endeavour.

She glanced at Mila. They both grew up in a big city, and their attachment to their Jewishness differed from mine. They just wanted to be left alone, without having a label. To go to Israel meant embracing the identity not popular in the Soviet Union.

"I worry about the mandatory military draft, even for girls. There's constant war there. I'm afraid." We both looked at Mila. She picked a napkin and put it back. It seemed to me she was buying time.

"I'm afraid too. Besides, Israel is a small country." After a pause, she added, "I'm not sure we would culturally fit there." Another pause, this one was long. "What's more, Israel is struggling to keep itself alive militarily and economically. We had enough of war and shortages."

"What other options do we have?" Rika looked at me.

"There are only three countries that would accept us as refugees." I used my fingers to emphasize this.

"First, the United States, second, Canada, and third, Australia. The latter two would gladly accept you, a young educated person. Our education and above all

136

our age would disqualify us. So, it's America. I am convinced, with luck, it would be the right choice. Just keep in mind, it's not a hundred percent guaranteed we will receive the refugee status."

I wasn't an ardent Zionist either, and the happiness of my family was the most important thing to me. The decision to go to America was unanimous. We believed America offered greater freedom and opportunities.

A woman's voice dragged me from the past to the present.

"I represent the Hebrew Immigration Aid Society, HIAS for short, to smooth the transition of Jews who chose to start their new life outside Israel." She was in her mid-thirties, tall and pretty with dark hair on the left side tucked behind her ear.

"We will take care of you here," she continued in perfect Russian with a Moscow accent, "and organize the next stage of your journey to Rome where you will wait for visas."

We were, as it often happened, behind the crowd. Mila urged me to get closer to the woman so I wouldn't miss a word. Elbowing my way through the thick crowd, I got so close to her I could smell her scent. She smelled of fresh air in a spring forest. Apparently, the ability to take a hot shower every day and perfume and makeup without problems available in the West played role in this. The crowd was anxious, shouting so many questions at the same time that it made my teeth rattle. "Where are you from? Are you from America? How long do we have to wait in Italy? Who will help us?"

"Wait a minute!" She flipped strands of hair out of her almond-shaped eyes and scanned the crowd until people went silent. She looked at us and smiled, "I will answer your questions. And if you have more questions, please, raise your hands."

"I'm from Moscow," she said after a brief pause. "I came here a few years ago when Gorbachev opened the door to Jewish emigration. By the way, he did the same for forbidden Christian minority sects, like Baptists. You may meet them here. Don't be surprised. We take care of them also." She stopped for a moment waiting for questions, but everyone kept silent.

"I was good with English and HIAS offered me work with Russian-speaking immigrants who started to come to Vienna in ever-growing numbers. English is important, spend time mastering it while you waiting for visas." A few hands went up.

"Wait," she continued. "The processing of applications takes a few months for America and a year or more for Canada or Australia. It takes time to learn where you would build your new lives. Applications may be denied."

At this moment, the shouting resumed as if she didn't explain to us how to ask questions. Now, I was sympathetic towards the crowd. I, along with my fellow immigrants, was taking a big risk. To come so close to our dream only to be told we might not come to America was a nightmare. We knew where we wanted to go, but we didn't know where we would end up. All we knew about the future was that we were Jews bound for America.

The woman raised her hand and remained silent until the noise subsided. "I don't know why a few people refused refugee status. My advice is, prepare well for the interview."

Dusk had fallen by the time we finished with all formalities and boarded the buses that waited to take us to what ended up being a dormitory. On the way, I looked at the marked roads, tidy country homes—the suburbs of Vienna were turning into the city with nice parks and magnificent buildings.

We disembarked, and here we were, with all our possessions packed in six suitcases, at the doorway of a dormitory and the free world, unprepared, as we would soon discover, for what immigration held in store for us. The wind whistled through few trees at the side of the building, a cool breeze for July. The building, frozen by decades of winters and parched by summers, looked like an old woman who gave up on her appearance. Inside it was worse, and, of course, no elevators. We schlepped our luggage upstairs, making a few trips. Creaking stairs with paint peeling from the handrails led us to the third floor. The floor, a gloomy suite of rooms, reminded me of Soviet residences. Tired and excited, we settled in our room sitting beside each other—overwhelmed, bewildered, and happy. I looked at Mila.

"What?" I said.

"It's so—"

"I don't care. We are one step closer to America."

"Yes—"

"What is a dilapidated dormitory, compared to our journey? America is the light at the end of a long tunnel. I would sleep with rats if that's what it takes."

The exchange was interrupted by the HIAS woman knocking at our door and directing us to a snack.

Chapter 26

I could tell we were coming to a kitchen. The familiar odour drifted into the corridor like an invitation to follow where it led. The odour hit me full force the moment I stepped through the door, the memorable hot greasy scents of frying potatoes and sausage. The combination of a kitchen-dining room had tables of various sizes and was softly lit. People quietly talked as they ate. Like a school cafeteria, the room wasn't quiet. People, for the most part, women, knew their way around and cooked on the row of ranges along the far wall that likely hadn't seen a fresh coat of paint in years.

"It smells of a Soviet dining hall," I said.

They say women have a better sense of smell than men. It seemed true because Mila said after a pause, "It smells of broken promises."

I blinked and brought myself back into the room. Rika scrunched her nose with inhaling and gave Mila a perplexed stare.

"Rika, what the look is about?" Mila reacted.

"'Broken promises' sounds scary." She kept wrinkling her nose as if she were trying to sniff the truth behind the remark.

A little boy, chased by an old grandmother, frolicked past us across the room. I looked around, trying to figure out who the people were. Although I didn't know anyone, most people looked familiar. I was surprised to see people with colours of hair ranging from blond to dark brown, flat cheeks, bulbous noses, and light-coloured eyes. They looked unmistakably Slavic compared to their Jewish compatriots. I figured they were Christians of the sects persecuted in the Soviet Union as the HIAS representative explained to us earlier. Although the 'H' stood for Hebrew, HIAS took care not only of Jews. I also noticed people with wavy black hair, narrow eyes. *Do they take care of Muslims also?* I found out that they were the Bukhara Jews from the Central Asian Soviet Republic of Uzbekistan. It was my first encounter with non-Ashkenazi Jews.

Intrigued, a couple of days later, I approached a Bukhara woman.

"How was your life there?"

"It was difficult." She befell silent. "It's easy for you," she said, "because your neighbours can't tell that you are Jewish by your looks. You look Slavic. As for us, they at once saw we are Jewish."

"To me, you look like Uzbeks." My eyes went wide. "And nobody mistook me for a Slav before."

Separated by thousands of years, we looked different—Russian-Jewish faces and Uzbek-Jewish faces. We were different; different branches with the same roots.

On the second day in Vienna, we were supposed to go for interviews by an office that processed Soviet émigrés. Worried about how we would find our way in an unfamiliar city, I asked a man who was here for a week,

"How to reach the office?"

"There is a metro here." He stared down at me. "It would take you close to the office. Just exit at this stop." He pointed to a spot on the city map we picked up in the lobby. "And follow the crowd of Soviet Jews." Responding to my confused expression, he added, "Don't lose sleep, you will recognize them."

"By the way," he said, "Buy tickets for public transportation that allow you to board any means of transportation for ten days. It would cost less and be more convenient than to pay for each ride."

It was great advice. It saved us money not only on necessary trips but allowed us to explore the city in our free time.

Walking from the metro, we took in the magnificent capital of the Austro-Hungarian Empire, which after WWI turned into the capital of a small non-aligned country at the crossroads of East and West. That's why we ended up in Vienna. Dozens of Soviet Jews were hurrying their way through morning Vienna as if trying not to be last in line. Following the people, we approached the office. I saw familiar faces from the Moscow airport. "Any news?" we asked each other, eager for good ones.

At the office, they gave us long forms to fill out and directed us to the tables. Translators walked around to help. One question was familiar, "State the reasons for leaving the Soviet Union." It would be a problem to put my whole life into two lines they afforded me if not for all the thinking I did trying to figure out the same thing. Without hesitation, I wrote: Anti-Semitism, lack of freedom, and harsh economic conditions.

The oral interview with a lot of treacherous questions followed. I still remember a few, others I forgot. Were you circumcised? Do you celebrate Jewish holidays? I was prepared for the tricky questions and just hoped the rest of my family would heed my warnings: "Don't tell you baked matzos for Purim. It's for Pesach (Passover), for Purim you bake Hamantaschen. And don't light a mezuzah on Hanukah. It's a menorah."

"And what is mezuzah?" Rika asked.

"Mezuzah is the little container with passages of the Torah that Jews affix to doorsteps of their homes." The images of my childhood home turned up in my head. "We had them at the door frames in our home. I remember my father kissed his fingertips and touched the mezuzah when he left or came back from his out-of-town job."

We made a few more trips to the office. One day, they made another attempt to persuade us to go to Israel. But the dice were cast. We combined those trips with exploring the city. One day we went to see the opera house. It was beautiful. Call me biased, but I thought the Odessa opera house was nicer.

In the middle of July 1989, we left Vienna for Rome by the train chartered by HIAS to transport Soviet refugees. The platform where we boarded the train was guarded by soldiers with automatic weapons and guard dogs. The guns looked small compared to the ones I remembered from my army days.

Vienna, Jews, trains, soldiers, dogs; did it look the same about fifty years ago?

"Why are the armed soldiers here?" Rika asked.

"I heard that about ten years ago, Palestinian terrorists tried to kill Jewish immigrants boarding a train."

"Can they attempt now?"

"That's why the soldiers are here." I tried to placate Mila.

Soviet Jews roiled, twisted, and elbowed to deposit their belongings onto the waiting train. Mila, Rika, and I worked furiously with our suitcases and sacks. They told us that we have only seven minutes to finish loading everything onto the train. I sent Rika inside so she would receive the luggage we would force through the open window of the compartment. I lifted the sacks onto my shoulder and, together with Mila, slid them along the outside of the train into Rika's hands. Each seemed heavier than the last.

When we entered the compartment, it was crammed with our stuff.

"The compartment is half the size," Mila said. "Say what you want about the Soviet Union, but the sleeping compartments there were bigger."

We were finally on a European train boring our way through the Alps. We rocked a little with the train, which raced through the mountains without concern for our worries. After the flats of Southern Ukraine, the picturesque mountains with tidy fields and accurate villages looked different from familiar landscapes.

Chapter 27

For logistical reasons, we were supposed to disembark at a railway station outside Rome. The day was clear and warm, with a sporadic breeze blowing from the river. Rika looked out the window and said, "The soldiers are not as threatening as in Vienna."

I recalled my relatives saying something like that about Italian soldiers during World War II.

"Okey, we don't have time. Now, we had to put our luggage onto the platform in just a few minutes before the train proceeds." The method we used to get the luggage into the train in Vienna was now reversed. I sent.

Mila and Rika out to stand beneath the window. I wrenched the suitcases and sacks from the floor and lowered them out the window.

We boarded buses that brought us to a hotel in Rome. While in Rome, Russian refugees shared information, above all about how to sell what we brought for sale and where to find rentals. HIAS expected us to move out from the hotel after a week.

"Tomorrow morning, someone will knock on your door," a fellow immigrant, who arrived in Rome five days earlier, said to me. "Don't be afraid. They are Soviet immigrants who are stuck in Italy and trying to make money to support their families by reselling to the locals what we brought from Russia," He also gave me approximate prices the merchandise went for. "And don't take Italian liras. Only American dollars."

The Soviet authorities prevented us from taking with us the meagre proceeds from selling our whole Soviet lives. They allowed only exchanging sixty rubles per person for dollars. The official exchange rate was sixty kopeks for a dollar. On the black market, it was five rubles for a dollar. We left all but penniless, but with suitcases with trinkets to sell. Permitted to leave, we were advised by fellow aspiring emigrants to spend whatever money left on any goods that could be sold to supplement the assistance we would get. No one knew if or when an American visa would be granted or why most people were accepted while others refused entrance.

The next morning, as the man told, at about nine o'clock, a knock at our door alerted us. We were dressed and prepared. Two men came in.

"What do you have to sell?" one of them asked without saying hello. Seeing the goods spread on the bed, both rushed ahead. They chose what they wanted. I used my Privoz experience to bargain. They were also experienced even more so. After agreeing on the price, one of them reached into his pocket and removed a billfold of Italian liras.

"No, I want dollars," I said as I was instructed.

Without a word, the man reached into another pocket and took out a billfold of dollars. He counted $250 and gave them to me. Before coming out of the door, the man asked. "Anything else you got?" I pointed to the bed. He wasn't interested in the remaining stuff.

HIAS wanted us out of the hotel in a week. The hotel cost a lot of money. During these seven days, we had to interview with the American consulate and find lodging outside Rome. While there, we tried to see as much of the city as possible walking the streets of Rome, and spent some money on excursions. It was difficult to believe that I saw the Coliseum and the Vatican. I had an additional important task, to find a rental fast if I wanted a roof over my family's heads.

During the first wave of emigration in the 1970s, several towns around Rome had been selected as suitable and affordable holding places for Jewish refugees for whom economic and freedom issues were more important than religious ones. The HIAS staff had told us we needed to find housing in one of those towns. They would still pay for rent, but we had to arrange it ourselves. We looked for accommodations in Ladispoli. There we were supposed to wait for refugee status to America. We would rent a room or apartment and wait anxiously for permission to come to America.

One day, I left my family near the rail station to explore the city and left by train for the town of Ladispoli.

"Find something, please," Mila said looking me in the eyes. Then she hugged me.

The hub of Russian activity in Ladispoli was Piazza Marescotti, close to the beach. The 'Russians' settled close to the Piazza in the central area of the town. The Piazza served as a social club, information centre, and bazaar. That's where

I decided to look for information about rentals in the city. When I arrived, I saw an old man holding a sign offering English lessons. A few men and women had spread blankets on the ground to display merchandise they brought from Russia. Most traded in linen, photo equipment, and tools. I strolled along to see what prices others were charging for the goods I still had. Then, I walked around looking at people and listening to the conversation. Most, it looked to me, just were there to kill time and exchange gossip as well as useful information. I joined them to get leads on apartments. I got none. The demand for cheaper rentals exceeded what the city had to offer. After an hour of wandering around, listening to conversations, and asking questions, I became desperate. *God help me. What will I say to Mila? We need to move.* "Don't come back until you find an apartment." Not these words Mila said to me before I left Rome but her pleading eyes were on my mind. My heart pounded through my chest as I looked around praying silently for someone to rescue me.

I stood with my outstretched palm above my eyes looking for a miracle. My body crooked as a question mark. I could swear someone had come behind me, yet hesitated to turn around for fear I would be wrong. Then, I felt a gentle touch on my shoulder. I jerked around.

"Yakov Isaakovich." I heard. That was the answer to my "prayer".

A fellow physics teacher from Odessa extended his hand.

"Victor Petrovich, what are you doing here?" I said.

"The same as you."

"But you are not Jewish. Or are you?"

"I am."

"Ryabchuk?"

"Yeah, yeah… I was blessed with the Ukrainian-sounded last name."

"You look upset, what's wrong?" he asked after I hugged him instead of shaking his hand.

"So glad to see you. Do you live here? I'm looking for an apartment."

I didn't know him well. We just met from time to time at teacher's conferences. But right now, he was my best friend in the world, my hope, and my present link to my Odessa life.

"You are in luck," he smiled. "I know of an apartment that just emptied. An Odessan family left yesterday for New York. They had a good room in a three-room apartment with two other families from Odessa. They are looking for—"

"Give me the address." I felt my face relaxed and my body releasing the tension.

He gave me the address and pointed to Via Italia, the central street going north from Piazza Marescotti.

"Talk to you later. A drink is on me." I hurried away.

I found the building just ten minutes from the Piazza and ran to the third floor. I spent a few moments catching my breath before knocking on the door. I banged at the door. At the sound of the hurried steps inside the apartment, I let the air from my lungs. A woman opened the door. She looked at me like I was KGB.

"I'm from Odessa," I said. "I am looking for a place to rent... please."

"Oh, do come in," her fearful frown turned into a welcoming smile. I took a good look at her. She was of average height, plump, and in her thirties. Her black hair and almond-shaped black eyes together with a familiar accent put me at ease.

"When did you arrive?"

"Just five days ago. And you?" I said.

"We are here for about a year," she said casually.

"That long!" My heart sank.

"Oh, no," she said looking at my face. "We are waiting for Australia; it takes a long time. If you are going to America, it usually takes, if they approve you, two to three months." She smiled. I smiled back, and then my smile widened into a grin.

"Let me show you the room."

"Oh, yes. Of course."

Why wait a year to go to Australia? I didn't ask, I wanted to see the room and have a place to live while waiting for a visa to America.

The apartment was large by Soviet standards—three rooms, a big kitchen, and a separate bathroom and shower. For three families in one apartment, it was important. In the Soviet Union, it wasn't rare that more than three families lived in a communal apartment with one bathroom without a shower. The room was a decent size with a king-size bed, a small table, and a few chairs. It had a closet. It was the first time I saw a closet. We usually had wardrobes in our apartments.

"Yes, I will take it."

We discussed the price—it was a third of the rent for the whole apartment. We could afford it.

"We will move in tomorrow. I'm so glad."

"I'm also glad to have fellow Odessans."

"Why wait a year for Australia, why not America?" The unasked question bothered me.

"In Australia, they help more."

"I will rush back to Rome to tell my family. So long."

"See you tomorrow."

We moved in the next day. Our room was a multipurpose space, a living room, and a family room during the day and a bedroom at night like back in the Soviet Union. An anecdote came to mind.

A factory worker in America shows his house to his Soviet colleague. "This is my room, this is my wife's, this is my daughter's, this is our dining room, then the guest bedroom…" The guest nods and says after a pause: "Well it's basically similar to mine. Only we don't have internal walls."

We stacked the suitcases high in one corner, clothes in the closet. We would be living off the allowance the HIAS paid each individual plus what I could earn selling the remaining merchandise we brought with us.

One day I went to the piazza to try to sell some things. I was a little embarrassed, but I found a spot and became a paddler. I spread a towel on the sidewalk and put out what merchandise we didn't get rid of in Rome—matryoshka dolls, tools, and lenses. Later, Mila and Rika came by.

"Did you sell anything?" Mila asked scanning the towel with the merchandise.

"Two matryoshkas and one lens," I said and reached into my pocket to draw out Italian bills, "my first sale." The few hundred liras I made didn't transform our time in Italy into a vacation.

A few months in Italy, in the summer, on the Mediterranean! It may be looked like a dream vacation. But it wasn't. Yes, occasionally we went to the beach. The locals avoided our beach where hundreds of immigrants were bathing in the sun, swimming, and, of course, eating. It reminded me of Odessa beaches where people spread big towels and covered them with food as if for a birthday party: boiled potatoes, schmaltz herring, sandwiches, and a rainbow of radishes, tomatoes, and cucumbers. They ate and fed children.

"Eat with bread," a mother pleaded with a toddler who turned his head away, "or you won't grow."

"Yeah, your peepee won't grow," the father interjected.

"Your parents should have fed you better," the mother snapped.

Typical Odessa.

Most days we filled not with beaches but with appointments, free English classes, markets, museums, and, of course, worry. Mila and Rika's fretting about the refugee status poisoned the 'vacation' for us. Tension filled our time in Italy. We left the Soviet Union with an exit visa stamped for Israel. We now had to apply for permission to settle elsewhere. Most of the world was closed to us. Our particular choices were limited to America… and Israel. There were applications and interviews to go through—and the spectre of being denied the coveted refugee status.

There were supermarkets in Ladispoli. Getting the apartment, we could afford, we barely could pay for much else. The amount of money we legally brought from the Soviet Union totalled about three hundred dollars. Combined with a few hundred dollars of the proceeds from the sales of goods we brought with us, they made up our whole capital. Life in Italy wasn't cheap and the money channelled through the relief agencies wasn't enough. We couldn't afford the supermarkets. Sometimes, farmers would bring fruits and vegetables and sell them on the central street. But the main food purchases we made at a big farmer market in Rome. Since I entered the Privoz market in Odessa for the first time, I'd loved markets. I put to good use the skills I acquired and honed at the Privoz. The whole point was to get there about an hour before closing when the sellers were negotiable to get rid of unsold products. Sometimes, at closing, an exhausted farmer added free overripe vegetables or fruits. Despite the language barrier, the tactics I used in Odessa worked in Rome. We communicated in limited English or by gestures, and later in rudimentary Italian. I still remember the phrase 'quanta costa'—how much. It wasn't easy to bargain in a foreign language, but I managed. Chicken or turkey wings quickly found their way onto our dinner table—it was all my family could afford. We sarcastically called them "The Wings of the Soviets," applying the name of the popular soccer team sponsored by the Soviet air force. Whenever I went there, I thought about the Privoz. For two months in Italy, we made a few trips to the market in Rome, usually combined with appointments or excursions.

My recollections of the time were bittersweet. Our lives were centred on waiting for acceptance. We knew well our point of departure but not necessarily our destination. Anxiety, an integral part of the refugee makeup, waited for us while we were waiting for our fate to be decided. No one knew if or when American visas would be granted and why some people were accepted while others refused entrance.

Our fate would be decided at a make-or-break interview with US consular officials in Rome. Despite the summer-warm beaches, life in the resort wasn't a holiday. We languished in the uncertainty of our future. There are only a few things worse than uncertainty.

After my English class one late sunny Friday afternoon, I came home to find Mila and Rika in our room. I entered the room and discovered a sad scene. Gloomy faces in the middle of the bright day were not a welcome sign. *Did someone die?*

"What happened?" my voice trembled.

Rika handed me a letter. It shook as though it was quivering in a breeze. Not knowing what to say, I reread it taking my time after I already knew what it meant. Basically, it said to call the HIAS office.

"It doesn't mean anything." I faked a smile, as my heart stopped in my throat and blood thundered in my ears.

"But papa, everyone says such a letter means the request to enter America was denied. What will we do now?"

Mila was silent. A tear rolled onto her cheek.

"I will call right now." I checked for change and hurried out to the phone booth at the corner. I called the number and got a recorded message, "The office is closed for the weekend and will reopen Tuesday because Monday is an Italian national holiday."

Three days? Three days! I wished to speed the clock to make the calendar pages flip.

On the way back I checked the cash we had at hand and started planning to cut expenses. It was the longest three days. I struggled to keep a positive attitude for my family's sake, but these were gloomy days. Nine o'clock Tuesday morning the three of us stood at the corner phone booth. I dialled the HIAS's phone number again.

"Good day." I thought about what to say next.

"Yes."

"I have a letter."

"Yes."

"What this letter is?"

After a pause, "What's your name?"

"Yakov Grinshpun."

"Okay. Wait a minute." I held my breath. "Your guarantor will be in Fort Lauderdale instead of New York as previously arranged."

"That is… all?" After she said yes, I put the receiver back without saying "Goodbye." The air left my lungs, and with a big smile, I turned to my family.

"Everything is okay." I pushed my shoulders back. "We are going to Fort Lauderdale instead of New York."

"What is Fort Lauderdale?" asked Rika. "And, where is it?"

"Have no idea. It doesn't matter. We are going to America!"

"Yes, it does," Rika said. "Let's go to the library and find out, can we papa?"

"You are looking kind of cheery, my dear," I looked at Mila.

"I'm doing much better." It seemed like, while I was talking to Rika, someone erased the worry from her face with a wet cloth.

"Call your cousin," she urged. "Find out what Fort Lauderdale is."

I dialled the number and a lady on the other end answered the call. I said, "Collect." We didn't have the money for an international call. My cousin's wife Evelyn answered. When I told her why I was calling, she explained to me what happened. I listened attentively and nodded saying uh-huh, uh-huh, uh-huh from time to time.

"Do they know what uh-huh means?" Mila interjected. I just waved my hand and continued listening. To me, Evelyn's voice was like music. Although I couldn't understand every word, I understood the gist of what she was telling. Finally, I asked the question that bothered my daughter and my wife.

"What is Fort Lauderdale, and where is it?"

"Oh, it's close by, just a few miles from Margate where we live." I could hear a smile in her voice even over the phone.

Replacing the receiver without a bang, I turned to my family and said,

"She told that Alan's sister because she couldn't take care of herself, moved from New York to a facility near them." They both continued looking and me. "And by the way, Fort Lauderdale is near Margate in Florida."

We went to the library, I asked for a map of the United States, and we searched for Fort Lauderdale. The city was just a tiny dot on the map. I wish we had Google back then. But Sergey Brin, the co-founder of Google, was only sixteen. He left the Soviet Union—where he wouldn't have been able to found Google—only ten years earlier.

"Let's celebrate a little," I said. "We can spend some money we made selling the merchandise we brought. Who knows if we will ever go back to Italy? Let's go and see something."

We were thirsty to see the world. Russian-Jewish "entrepreneurs," who were refused the entry visa and settled in Italy, offered cheap trips to three locations in the country. The excursions were a fraction of what foreign tourists would pay for a regular tour. The tours included transportation, lodging, meals, and museum tickets. Who cared that the buses were not comfortable, that instead of glossy brochures they just handed out a piece of paper with typed information, that the hotels we stayed in were one-star at best? We would see the same things in those places as the tourists who paid many times over what we paid. We, by a hair's breadth, could afford one excursion of the three offered and used most of the money we made. We never regretted it. Florence, San Marino, and Venice looked like the best choice. To see the statue of Michelangelo's David in Florence, the beautiful palaces and canals in Venice, and the unbelievably charming San Marino was worth every penny we spent on the trip.

In Florence, we stood a long time before the statue of David in front of the Uffizi museum.

"I never thought it's so big," Rika said.

"And beautiful," Mila added. "It took a genius to make it."

"Have you ever dreamed to see this?" I asked Mila in Venice. She just smiled. San Marino was a fairy tale.

Soon after we returned from the trip, I checked the mail and saw an official-looking envelop. I ran up the stairs to our room and waved the letter in front of Mila and Rika.

"What is it?" Mila said. "Is it from immigra—"

"It is from immigration!" Rika sprang from the bed. "I can tell from your face, papa."

"It's the decision," I shouted, "who has a lucky hand?"

"Me, papa, let me," Rika extended her hand, and I handed her the letter. She took what seemed like a very long time to tear it open.

I didn't move, and I saw Mila also not moving. It was like we both were characters in a science fiction movie, frozen in time, unable to even breathe.

"Yea, yes, yes!" Rica said.

Mila jumped from her chair, her hip banging into another chair and almost knocking it over. I hugged Rika, then Mila. They hugged each other. I took the letter and read it not missing one word. I exhaled. "We... Are... Going... to America." The coveted refugee status in my hand. That's when the true Italian vacation began.

September 6, two months to the day that we embarked at the awful Soviet plane, we, at four in the morning, were boarding a bus for Rome International Airport.

"Look," Rika said as we stepped into the plane. "It has three rows of seats."

Our seats were in the right row. Mila wanted the aisle seat, and Rika liked the window. I didn't have a choice. Rika moved first, then I took my seat, and when Mila lowered herself into the seat, she said, "Not like the small compartments of the Vienna train."

"Different from the Soviet plane." I grinned, "And the stewardesses look nice."

Mila rolled her eyes, so I turned to Rika, "What do you like about the plane?"

"It's so clean and smells nice." She smiled and put her hand on the button. "I already tried to recline and, you know, it works as it supposes to."

On the long flight over the Atlantic, the contrast between the Soviet plane and the American one made me think about the country I left and the country I was going to. Although the giddiness of making it to America carried me for a while, I started to worry. *Did the bittersweet time in Vienna and Italy portend what was awaiting us? Had I made the right decision?* I knew what was bad in the old country and the miserable future that awaited my family over there. The regime pushed us on the Soviet plane. The American promise pulled us on this one. To reassure myself and to placate my mind, I made an inventory of what I knew. I began to contrast the countries, not just the planes. I summoned what I had learned about the United States. The Soviet reality I knew well.

In many aspects, the United States and the Soviet Union were complete opposites. Just look at the names of both: **U.S.** and **S.U.** Capitalism vs Communism. We used to joke that in a capitalist society, it's the exploitation of man by man, and in a communist one, it's the exact opposite. In the Soviet Union people who had power had money. In the United States, people with money had power. *At least in the United States, we would have the opportunity to earn* *enough money to have a decent life, I thought.* I could've stopped right there, but it was a nine-hour flight. And contrasting felt better than worrying.

While America built its prosperity through freedom, Russia sought stability through autocracy; America's heroes were businessmen, Russia's were writers who examined the human soul with intensity. Writers fed my soul, but they didn't put food on my table. In America, the individual was supreme. In Russia, they celebrated the supremacy of the communal over personal. That's why in Russian the 'You' is capitalized, in English, it's the 'I'—stark choice of different views of human nature and aspirations. Most significant they were different in the most important thing. America guaranteed freedom and pursuit of happiness. This ensued a question: "Do they have something in common?" I tried to compare the countries but couldn't find any similarities. It left no doubt in my mind what a rational person would choose. I relaxed, but not for long.

"We have reached the cruising altitude of forty thousand feet." We were crossing the Atlantic on a Rome-JFK plane. We were forty thousand feet up in the air as they announced. About thirteen thousand meters, I calculated. Another problem, I thought, to learn the new non-metric system. At this thought, I stopped and looked around.

A few men dressed as I imagined businessmen would—suits and ties. I thought about the five suits in our luggage and tried to picture myself as a businessman who provides for his family. My imagination didn't work.

I began thinking about the future. Soon we would land in the free world. I didn't wish for free staff. What I wanted is to be free to pursue happiness for my family. That's what we lacked in the place we left behind. Every immigrant who comes to America expects something. I was prepared to work hard. We don't abandon family, friends, careers, and graves of our ancestors without the hope of something good to be found in America. We were short in the Soviet Union of opportunity. Opportunities were for the Party elite who made decisions for us.

Our plane dipped its wings as it approached New York, and I caught sight of futuristic high-rises casting long threatening shadows. The future looked at us through the window as the plane descended. The plane shed more altitude. After the landing gear hit the runway and bounced to a stop, Rika said:

"You brought us to America."

"No, it's the plane," I quipped not knowing what to say.

"We were given new lives," Mila said. "A stork brought us to America."

153

"No, it's you," Rika took a glance at Mila and settled her eyes on me. "But I wish a stork brought me here." We laughed.

In the spotlessly clean labyrinth of JFK International Airport, we found ourselves on the doorsteps of our new country. *Is this happening to me? Am I about to arrive in America? Is it just me, or does every immigrant feels the same excitement and fear facing the unknown?* I looked at Mila and Rika. They looked at me looking as bewildered as I felt.

An official from HIAS met us and rushed us to the connecting flight to Fort Lauderdale. On the way to the gate, I had my eyes wide open. People hurried around. Others sat around spotless tables eating or drinking coffee. Obedient lines of passengers quietly waited for their flight. I never saw so many smiling faces. *Why are all of them smiling? Doesn't anybody worry about customs?*

When I asked for a toilet, our guide directed me to a place with a strange name—restroom. I was too excited to need a rest. In the restroom the floor gleamed, the sinks sparkled, and the hand-dryers (the first time I ever saw one) whirred. It was a place where one can rest. I thought of the disgusting public toilets in the Soviet Union that nobody called restrooms. This restroom smelled of nothing, which was strange. Back in Russia, the sense of smell was habitually attacked by the odour of sweat and unwashed clothes, boiled cabbage in cafeterias, and exhaust from trucks running on leaded petrol. Public toilets were a separate category.

"How was it?" Mila asked when I returned.

"Go and check. Both of you."

When they came back, their faces told me all I needed to know. As we continued walking, Rika touched me by the elbow and whispered, "What is it?" I looked where she pointed with her eyes. A few men in strange attire—long coats, fur hats, and long beards. I turned to the HIAS woman, "What is it?"

"Hasidic Jews," she answered.

I never saw anything like that. Hasidic Jews were only vaguely known to me at that time. I never saw even a man in a yarmulke on the streets of Odessa. I struggled to bring myself back into the 20th century.

At the gate to the Fort Lauderdale flight, our chaperon approached a group of people and talked to a man. She turned to us and said, "This is the Rykman family. They are flying to Fort Lauderdale also."

Alex and Emma Rykman with their two toddler sons were from Leningrad. She was a woman with nice curves, like Mila, tanned skin, and a full-lipped mouth made for a smile. He looked intelligent.

"Where you are going from Fort Lauderdale?" I asked after we shook hands.

"To Coconut Creek where our relatives live," Emma said. "And you?"

"To Margate, we will stay with my cousin." I was disappointed. "Hope we would be able to see each other."

In Russia, towns were at least miles away. Who knew that in South Florida towns didn't separate? One side of the street was Coconut Creek the other was Margate. Our relatives' condominiums were a few blocks apart. Alex and Emma became our friends.

We changed planes in Charlotte, North Carolina. We didn't leave the airport. We weren't in real America yet. The plane hung suspended in mid-air somewhere over the East Coast of America; clouds beneath and the starry sky above. Our lives hung, suspended in the air, like an unfinished bridge. All we knew about our future was that we were citizens of no country and Jews given a chance to become Americans.

Part V
Becoming American

Chapter 28

The plane started the descent. Clouds obscured the stars as our plane began its final approach into Fort Lauderdale. Emerging beneath the cloud, the sudden view of the sprawling metropolis took my breath away—miles and miles of lights. I had never flown at night before and was impressed by the sea of light to the right contrasted by the sea of dark to the left. *What would our lives look like?*

I will never forget the date. It's September 6, 1989, and Fort Lauderdale International Airport is the fourth airport of the day. Soon we will be away from airports and into real America. The HIAS did take care of us from the touch-down in Vienna until the touch-down in Fort Lauderdale. We and our new friends, the Rykmans, disembarked.

"What do we do now?" Mila asked. I looked around, but Alex noted first and pointed to a young woman with pieces of paper with our last names in each hand.

"You are?" the woman said to me. I think it wasn't a problem for her to recognize 'Russians'.

"Grinshpun," I pointed to the paper in her right hand.

"So, you are Rykman," she waived the other paper at Alex.

"My name is Anya," she said. "I'm the representative of the Jewish Family Service of the Jewish Federation of Broward County." The federation took over from HIAS.

I looked at her again. She was of average height, not skinny, with short hair, and a face that reminded me of Odessa women.

"Where are you from, guys?" Anya asked.

"We were living in Odessa." To my surprise, Rika took the initiative.

"Oh, I'm from Odessa too." Anya smiled.

"And you are?" Anya turned to Emma.

"We are from Leningrad."

"When did you come here?" Mila asked.

"Ten years ago," Anya said.

"Did you come straight to Florida?" I put the accent on the 'I'—the Russian way.

"We had moved to Florida five years ago from up north," Anya stressed the 'o'. She looked at her watch and said, "Your relatives are waiting for you, let's move."

We went to the baggage claiming area. Anya guided us towards a group of two elderly couples sitting on a bench. They stood up as we draw near. One of the men looked vaguely familiar. Black hair sprinkled with grey, conservatively cut. He had a tanned face, green eyes, strong nose, and thin lips. He pointed a finger at me and said something in English.

"He says that he figured out that you are his cousin because you are bald as your father was," Anya interpreted. I touched my hairless scalp. It was my first cousin, Alan. Seventy years past since he last saw my father when he left Russia at the age of nine. Next to him was his wife Evelyn. The other couple was Emma's relatives.

We went through the introductions; talked or tried to for a while. After all the excitement, kissing, and hugging, Anya said: "It's getting late. Let's go home. You have a day or two to rest. I'll call you when to come to the Jewish Federation," she turned to the Americans. "You know where to go."

After claiming our luggage, we proceeded for the door to our new life. The door slid open by itself. On this hot and humid September day, my wife, my daughter, and I made our first step to America. As we stepped through the door into a wall of heat, the famous words of Neal Armstrong when he made the first step on the moon came to my mind. "One simple step for a man—"

"And a gigantic step for our family," Rika finished. *She is already more assertive in America*, I thought.

We crossed the multilane road and stepped through an opening inside a multi-storeyed windowless structure. The heat and humidity were like in a Russian steam bath. Autumn had already begun, but my face was on fire in the scorching air. The humidity weighed on me like a heavy blanket, and the air was so thick on my arms, it felt like sleeves.

"What is it?" I asked Anya.

"It's a garage."

"What?" I had never experienced such weather and had never seen a parking garage. You were lucky to even have a car in Russia. I had a feeling it is only the beginning of discovering new and mysterious things.

"I'll bring the car," Alan said. Emma's uncle left with him. In a few minutes, Alan exited from a big silver luxurious car. I thought it was a Rolls Royce I heard of back in Russia. We brought our luggage to the back of the car. "Oldsmobile," I read. Automobile means the same thing in Russian, so, maybe this was an automobile for old people. We put our luggage in the oversized trunk and took our seats. The heat followed us inside. Alan pushed a button and cool air began filling the car. It was my first encounter with air-conditioning. I knew of this invention, but I thought it was only for buildings.

We exited the airport onto a six-lane highway, the like of which I'd never seen before. Wow, what a sight. The ride was smooth, the tires whispered. The road was flat as glass. Lights separated the lanes.

"How do they make the separation lanes visible at night?" I asked.

"Reflectors," Alan said.

As a physics teacher, I felt embarrassed not having figured that out myself. Next, we were, for the first time for us, on an overpass, suspended in mid-air. Unbelievable, amazing view; overpasses above, overpasses below, endless lights on all sides, and tall buildings in distance. I glanced at Mila and Rika. I thought I had the same impression on my face.

"What is that?" I pointed to the buildings.

"Downtown," Evelyn said.

I knew the word down, and I knew the word town, I didn't understand what downtown means but was embarrassed to ask. In about half an hour the six-lane road changed into a four-lane one that narrowed to two. In a while, we turned into a development called Palm Springs. When we got to Alan's apartment, we met his daughter, Barbara, and her family. While the women prepared a light supper, Alan showed us the apartment. From my perspective, it was a luxury—two bedrooms, a living room, and an enclosed porch—four rooms not to count the kitchen and foyer.

After eating and small talk—small as our English was—we went to sleep after one of the longest days in our lives. Tomorrow our new life will begin. The past had been left behind, and the future was enticing.

It was early the next morning, not long after dawn had broken, and light had started to seep in through the curtains. Because of the time difference, I woke up early despite being tired. I trudged to the bathroom, and after, went onto the porch and looked outside. The sun barely cracked the black of the night. I could see a seam of dawn starting to build. It was still a whisper. Well-manicured ground and strange trees that I recognised as palm trees I saw in movies. I opened the sliding glass window, inhaling the morning air. It was so thick with moisture I thought I could almost see it. I could smell the sweet mixture of fresh-cut grass and quiet.

Later in the day, Alan and Evelyn's friends came to see us.

"Nice to meet you," they said.

"Good afternoon," I answered with a greeting I remembered from my school years.

"How are you?" one lady asked me.

Summoning my few words of English, I tried to tell how I felt.

"Just say 'Good'," Evelyn cut in.

"When people ask, 'How are you?'"—she took me aside—"always say 'Good'. Do they want to know how you are? No. Anybody who asked, only did so in anticipation of 'Good'."

At this point, I remembered an Odessa *anekdot*.

-Boris, why don't you ask me how am I?

-Rosa, how are you?

-Oy, don't even ask.

Evelyn continued our education in the evening. "When you meet people in the condominium, you have to greet everyone, and I mean everyone, and preferably ask how they are." She added, "Our neighbours and friends were intrigued by your story from the very time we received your first letter."

We had to learn to ask everyone, even strangers, how they were doing, and when asked, our answer always had to be "Good," even if it's not true. Eventually, I got so tired that I invented an answer, "It's too early in the day, I haven't decided yet." At least, it started a conversation. In the meantime, we dutifully greeted everyone we met although we felt uncomfortable doing it. When we caught people's eyes, they smiled at us. I never suspected that people can have so many and so white teeth. We were not sure how to respond. It was a new experience for us. Back in Russia, we tried to avoid looking strangers in the eyes. Even when we by chance did, we didn't smile. Russians are less likely to smile at strangers, they waste no smiling muscles. There is even a Russian proverb on the topic: "Smiling with no reason is a sign of stupidity." Americans grin at you with a plastic smile even when they hate you, but when passing you, the smile slides off their faces like a mask. It switches on and off as if by an eye

162

contact detector. To this day, I have to remind myself to smile back at people, and sometimes I forget. When I meet unsmiling people, I know that they are immigrants. I could recognize Russians at once by their facial expression. Their faces are not just unsmiling but stiff, lips pursed sternly, and eyes suspicious. Besides, their wear looked like a refugee from the Soviet Union of the 1950s— men in ill-fitting trousers and women in cotton dresses and knitted cardigans left no doubt they are fellow Russians. I try to smile at people so they won't recognize a Russian, most of the time in vain. Of course, it relates to older people, the young generation became well assimilated. Many of the ex-Soviet children became doctors and lawyers, engineers and programmers, entrepreneurs and innovators.

Chapter 29

Three days after our arrival, someone from the Jewish Family Service called.

"We are going to the Federation tomorrow at 11 A.M.," Alan said. It couldn't be at night, so I figured out that A.M. means in the morning. I was doing a lot of figuring lately.

Alan drove us to the Jewish Federation. Evelyn came along.

"Oh, you have a subway here. Maybe we'll be able to go to places by ourselves," I said when I saw a sign "SUBWAY."

"Oh no, it's a chain. They sell sandwiches." Evelyn laughed.

Why a chain?

We stopped at a red light. I sat behind the driver and looked at cars.

"You have to tell the people in the car next to us that their car leaks. Look, the water is coming underneath the car," I said. It meant the car would overheat. They both laughed.

"It's an air conditioner," Alan explained.

We arrived at the Federation and got off. The sky above echoed the flatness of the Florida landscape. Clouds listlessly changed shapes. One of them looked like a smiling face, a good omen. Palm trees swayed in a light breeze, their fronds whispering a gentle song.

We took the elevator and met Anya in her office. After exchanging pleasantries in English and Russian, she said, again in both languages: "Tomorrow, at 10 A.M., you have an appointment with Dr Sherman for a medical exam. He won't charge you. Here is the information." She handed Alan a business card. "The doctor is a Russian man who came to the United States ten years ago."

Was he smarter or luckier than us?

"I also made you an appointment at the Social Security office." Anya gave a printout to Alan.

"Why do we need security in the United States?" Rika whispered to me.

"Maybe we would figure it out when we got there." I didn't know and decided not to ask.

It looked like the whole month of September would be dedicated to different appointments, certainly making a lot of discoveries along the way. Everything was new, and lessons would be numerous.

Mila shushed us when Alan, on our behalf, asked, "What about a green card?"

"They'll have to wait a year until they can apply for the card," Anya answered.

"What is a green card?" I said.

"It makes you a permanent resident of the country," she explained.

"Why it's called green?" Rika whispered again.

"We will figure it out when we receive it?" I whispered back.

"So, what would it do for us?" Mila said.

"It can do a lot," Anya said. "For example, Rika would have to pay a lot less for college as a Florida resident." After a pause, she added, "The rest I'll explain later."

"In Russia, I didn't have to pay anything," Rika said. "They even paid me a stipend."

"This is not Russia." Alan's answer stopped the discussion.

We went to the doctor the following day. It was a small storefront office with one doctor, one nurse, and one receptionist, who said, "Sit down. The doctor will be with you soon."

It wasn't a clinic like in Russia. I understood now why in Russia it was called a polyclinic, poly meaning many. My district polyclinic was a three-story grey concrete box. Long corridors split each floor in half with numerous doors on each side. That's where we spent hours waiting to be seen by a doctor. There were two receptionists there and dozens of doctors, including specialists. All the employees wore white coats.

After a while, a casually dressed man came in and said, "Privet, I'm Dr Sherman, but you can call me Sasha." The doctor didn't have a white coat on. "I will examine you," he pointed to a young lady in a strange uniform that looked to me like a pair of pyjamas and also without a white coat, "after the nurse will

165

take all your necessary information and vitals. By the way," he added, "She doesn't speak Russian."

"I'm Stephanie," the nurse introduced herself. She was attractive. Her skin was light olive and her hair as black as a raven's, with split-curls at her ears. She not only looked different from Soviet nurses, but she smelled not like them.

"How are you?" she asked.

"I am good," I said. "But I have high blood pressure. And also—"

"It's okay," Alan said. "Just follow her directions."

At that moment, I recalled what Evelyn told me to do when asked such a question.

"Now we will take your weight," she pointed to the scales.

After all three of us stepped on the scale, Stephanie took a thermometer and, when I just looked at her, said, "Open your mouth." When I pointed to my armpit, she shook her head and repeated with a smile, "No, open your mouth."

I was perplexed, but she was not.

"And now urine analysis," she said when we were done with the temperature.

We blankly looked at her. "Analiz mochi." She smiled and quickly added, "That's all I know in Russian." She was all smiles.

The word analysis sounded similar in both languages and had to clue me, but it didn't. In a few minutes, the doctor entered. He asked questions, listened to our answers, and took notes. After that, he listened to our hearts and lungs. He gave us a clean bill of health.

"You wouldn't have to worry about health insurance for a while," Alan said. "It's good."

I didn't ask why it was good.

The next day, we went to the Social Security office. A black woman greeted us and started the paperwork.

We presented our visas and she copied the information.

"Nationality?" She said, returning the visas. The word sounded close enough to a Russian.

"Jewish," I answered.

"No," she didn't smile. "That's your religion. What country did you come from?" Thanks to residual English from my school years, despite her accent, I've got that question right.

"Russia. The Soviet Union."

"So, your nationality is Russian."

166

I started to say something, but Rika stopped me. "I think the word nationality means here what country you are from. Not what it meant in Russia."

"But in my Soviet passport on the fifth line "Nationality," the authorities identified me as Jew."

"I think it meant ethnicity," Rika said. I just shook my head.

I was never afforded the right to call myself Russian or Ukrainian when I lived in the USSR. If people would consider me either, it would make my life easier—from entering college to securing a good job to visiting brotherly socialist countries. All of a sudden here they called me a Russian when it was of no benefit to me, maybe even detrimental. The lady asked more questions, wrote down my answers.

"This is an application for a Social Security card and assistance," she said. I had gotten used to not asking too many questions. I should have asked about the assistance.

In the evening our friends, Alex and Emma, called to find out how the appointment went. I told them the story.

"You know," Alex said, "there's an anecdote in the Russian community about a man filling out paperwork. On the line Nationality, he answered like you, Jewish." He giggled. "And on the next question about sex he answered—three times a week. As the story goes, when he submitted the paperwork, he was told that he had to write on the sex line male or female. He answered, 'It doesn't matter to me.'" In Russian, 'sex' didn't mean gender.

Was I Russian or Jewish? Could I call myself American? It was confusing.

Chapter 30

A while later, I went to a bank for the first time by myself. When I approached the bank teller, she said, "Hello. How are you?"

"Good."

"How can I help you?"

"I want to put money in the bank."

"Deposit, then."

"You have an accent," she said to me while working on the computer.

"Really?"

"Yes, and a heavy one. What are you?"

"I'm Russian," I answered, remembering my first appointment in the Social Security office.

It didn't sound real like my answer to my niece's question didn't, on my last day in the Soviet Union about why I was leaving. On my way home, I, once again, tried to find the answer to a difficult question.

When I came home, Mila and Rika sat on the couch, reading. I asked Mila, "Who are you?" She looked at me.

"I'm not crazy. Are you Russian, Ukrainian, Jewish, or American? I told to the bank teller that I am Russian. But I am not."

"My dear," she said. "You have enough problems to waste time and energy on thinking about this nonsense." She resumed reading.

"Are you an American?" I asked Rika who listened to our conversation.

"Sort of," she shrugged and also returned to the book. Their answers didn't help.

As I assimilated into the new world while retaining elements of the old, I had to continuously redefine my identity. Who am I? I never before tried to scrutinize my life in those terms. I didn't need to. In astrology, if I believed in it, if I had to choose a zodiac sign for myself, it would be immigration. Since I settled in America, I lived a Russian-American life; with years passing, more American and less Russian. At any given moment of my immigrant life, I was to varying degrees a synthesis of both worlds. I embraced the new free world while still remembering how to take apart and reassemble the AK-47. Is the trauma of immigration ever going away? I left Russia. But did Russia leave me? Identity is a funny thing for someone like me. Born in Ukraine. Culturally and linguistically Russian. Labelled Jewish by the former Soviet Union. In a way, calling me a Soviet-American makes sense, but no. The Soviet Union no longer exists and besides, I hate the word Soviet. I continued thinking about my identity and came up with an all-encompassing answer that included all my identities.

Next, when I went to the bank, Mila went with me. It was the same teller. The conversation began as it was before, but then I said: "You know, the last time you asked me who I am, I answered 'Russian'. It's not right. I'm a Russian-speaking Jew from Ukraine." I grinned and she frowned.

"Stop it." Mila touched me and said in Russian.

After further consideration, when I had fully completed the journey through my complex identity, I came up with an answer to my satisfaction, "I'm an American." Yes, I'm an American. Not Russian-American, not Soviet-American, just plain American. America is my country, not Russia. My family, as well as my friends, is all here or in Israel. Being a Russian Jew, becoming an American Jew, and finally feeling like a Jewish-American.

Deciding that I am an American, I also had strong Jewish roots. I never felt a Jewish-Russian. For me what happens in Israel is more important than what happens in Russia. I identify myself as American one-hundred percent, sort of. But with my vodka-thick accent, I couldn't pretend I had no connections to Russia. As they say, you can take a man out of Russia, but you can't take Russia out of the man; at least not entirely. Russia inked into my soul like a tattoo. And the permanent tattoo is permanent. Maybe it's more appropriate to call us Russian-speaking. Even if I would like to call myself a Russian back in the old country, I couldn't. Here I could, but, at the moment that I write this, it's uncomfortable to call myself Russian in America like it was calling myself a Jew in Russia. In the United States, the feeling of not belonging was never as desperate and hopeless as it had been in the Soviet Union. The American part of my Russian-Jewish-American identity was the one that kept me anchored through immigration. If people weren't satisfied with "I'm an American," I could tell them more of my story. But I found that most people did not care about all that. They were just making conversation like asking about the weather. None of

169

my documents here list my ethnic origin or religion here, and I do not have to write it in any application. In America, I had the freedom to reinvent myself. It's my decision and right how to identify myself. I realised that identity is defined by how you feel and nationality is defined by borders.

Being an American who was immersed in Russian culture for many decades, I drew the best of both worlds, inheriting the sensitive Russian soul and the American dream. I didn't try to recreate my old life. Arguably, I am more American than the majority of Russian-speaking immigrants because I immersed myself in American life as much as I could. I read a lot about American history and culture and probably know more about American history than the average American does. And I spent countless hours mastering English.

After those considerations, it took me a while to realise that being an immigrant, despite what you believe or want to believe, means living with your soul and heart split in half. Well. Maybe not in half, nevertheless split. It's my destiny to live my whole life with a split. It's my destiny to live my whole life not being whole. In the Soviet Union for one reason, here for a different one. Split soul, I think, is the hidden heart of every immigrant's story. I've learned that split hearts and split souls never quite become whole. I felt caught in no-man's-land full of mines that separated my Russian past and my American present. Often, not knowing what the next steps would bring.

Many influences affected my perception of identity. One part was here, in my new country, the other was back in Odessa. My adopted country gave me so much—support, protection, and opportunity. I was full of gratitude but didn't fall in love with the country yet. The longer I live in America, the deeper my roots grew into the new soil. Though the wound of the separation begins to scab, the scar will always remain—Russian language, mentality, culture, and influences. Immigration is never easy.

By and large, I like my present life. America makes me forget that I'm adopted. I am living a second act now, different from the first.

Chapter 31

In the beginning, I was more 'Russian' and needed a lot of help. The first years, the first months in particular, of immigration are a curious and painful experience. In a new country, surrounded by people with unfamiliar customs with whom you cannot communicate right, it's a shock. Different habits, different languages, and your jokes were not understood here. I liked to joke and thought I was good at that. You feel like a boor, even though you have read all of Dostoevsky and Tolstoy and many other writes that most Americans never heard of, including the American ones. I lived more than half of my life in Russia, I've read all the books you can think of (government allowed, of course) and learned things that I didn't need to know. Did it help me to start my life anew? No. We needed the training because the Communist system handicapped us. We had no clue what a mortgage, credit card, or bank account was. The Jewish Federation paid for three months of our rent and provided social services and training. Anya helped us to open a checking account. One day she brought a check and a deposit slip and showed us how to fill them out. Such basic activities as opening a bank account, shopping in a supermarket, and buying a car were new and unfamiliar. It was a culture shock, an economic shock, and a mental shock. Some absorbed this shock better than others. You either adapt little by little or go through a major breakdown in the first few months.

We were thankful for the help from the local Jewish community. And we were thankful to American Jews for struggling non-stop against the Soviet giant 'to let my people go'. But many of us couldn't be grateful in the way our Jewish sponsors desired. Of course, we went to the synagogues when we were invited. In a few weeks, we attended the High Holidays services, and it was fascinating. We'd never seen anything similar. But most of us couldn't observe what had for so long been only a dangerous liability. In Russia, overcoming our Jewishness was a matter of preservation. It has been impressed into our brains and become instinctual. Together with our American benefactors, we discovered that instincts run deeper than conscious thoughts.

American Jews expected us, like the Jewish immigrants from the turn of the 20th century, to be either ardent Zionists like those who went to Palestine or to be like their grandparents who came to America from the shtetls. We were neither and failed to fit into non-Soviet notions of Jewishness. Unlike the religious Jews of the past, most of us were well-educated city dwellers with little religious feelings. At times, we had to pretend. It frustrated both sides and disenchanted some of the American Jews who had fought so hard for their oppressed fellow Jews. Some even labelled us as heretics and traitors to their Jewish heritage. Some indeed said, "These are Russians. They're not really Jewish." It's funny, I thought; non-Jewish Americans usually considered me Russian. That I was Jewish usually was an afterthought... but fellow Jews? In Russia, we were Jews, not Russians. And here we were, all of a sudden "Russians," not Jews. In Russia, they called us traitors because we were Jewish, here because we weren't Jewish enough. These experiences made me understand what any minority person—be it a person of colour, a gay, or a person that doesn't fit—feels. No one called me Russian in Russia. To become Russian, I had to come to America. Over there, I was a Jew among Russians; here, I became a Russian among Jews. We were, largely, a misunderstood group among Jewish Americans.

I'm not a traitor, and so are my fellow Russian-speaking émigrés. As products of an anti-religious (officially) and anti-Semitic (in practice) society, we are mostly non-observant, so we fail to fit neatly into the non-Soviet notion of Jewishness. We weren't escaping the country for freedom to worship. We did it for the freedom to pursue happiness. Our immigration seemed more motivated in partaking in the fruits of capitalism than the rites of Judaism. We are Jews with different experiences that hadn't lived as comfortably as our American brethren. Most of us had forgotten almost everything about the Jewish religion, but we hadn't forgotten that we were Jews. The Soviet system frowned on Judaism and other forms of religion, but mostly at our ethnicity. Most of us express our Judaism, or maybe it's better to say Jewishness, through the celebration of Jewish social and cultural heritage, not through religion. I belong to the majority. My encounters with Judaism and American culture are shaped and coloured by the intellectual and social training I received in Soviet school and college. That's why I and other 'nominal' Jews found it difficult when we arrived in the United States, to relate to English-speaking religious Jews. While a small percentage of us learned and accepted the Jewish faith while in America, most followed no particular religion but still being Jewish and following some Jewish traditions.

A part of the local Jewish community understood this and concluded that the Federation, although with the best intention, not always made the right decisions in helping us. They decided to find out what our problems are. At a meeting they convened, I was naïve enough to express those thoughts and talked about what we need. The mainstream Jewish community was not appreciative of this. One of the problems was the English language. The courses they advised us to attend were of no help in mastering the language.

"You know," I said. "At my age to hope to become a teacher, I have to go to college to learn the language. But I can't afford." I felt my cheeks flush, and I shifted my gaze downward. After a pause, I added, "In New York government pays for English lessons in community colleges. They even pay a stipend."

"So, you don't have the money," an elderly man said. I nodded.

"I will pay for you," he said.

"What?" I licked my lips. That was the only answer I could come up with.

"I will pick you up tomorrow, and we will go to the Broward Community College and I will pay for your English classes."

"Thank you," I said, holding tears back.

The next day, as promised, he picked me up and drove to the college.

"Where you from?" he said.

"I'm from Odessa. It's in—"

"I know where Odessa is. Where you born there?"

"No, I was born in a shtetl about a hundred miles from Odessa."

"Was the shtetl under the Nazi occupation?"

"Yes."

"So, how your family stayed alive?" He glanced at me. His eyes were wide open. I told him the story that I learned about my family's survival.

"So, you are a Holocaust survivor."

"Oh no. I was only about three months old when the Red Army liberated the shtetl."

"You still are a Holocaust survivor," he nodded a few times.

"What are your problems with the language?" he said, as we approached the college.

"My biggest problem vocabulary," I said, putting the accent on the 'u' in the word. I had to repeat it three times until he figured out what I meant.

"Hopefully the college will help you."

At the college, he helped me to enrol and paid for the English classes for two semesters. It was twice a week for two hours. It did help me. Tremendously. After so many years, I don't remember his name. I wish I could mention it here. I remember the names of the boys who assaulted me when I was at school and don't remember the name of the man who did such a mitzvah for me. I wouldn't be where I am now if not for him.

At the first English lesson, I realised that vocabulary wasn't my main problem.

We began with introductions. A lot of students had accents, not just me, and were from different countries. A lot of names didn't sound American. When a young beautiful girl from Brazil introduced herself as Sara, my eyes went wide and my mouth twisted. *A young girl, Sara? Isn't she ashamed of her name?* In Russia, all girls from my generation whose names were Sara changed their names to any Russian-sounded name that started with an 'S'. In their passports, they remained Sara's. And no Jewish girl was named Sara afterward. When my turn came, I introduced myself as Jacob, the English version of the original Yakov, and told them that I came from the Soviet Union.

"What part of the Soviet Union?" the professor asked.

"Ukraine."

"So, you are Ukrainian."

"No, I'm Russian," I said after a short delay.

Leaving the country, you grew up in and learning to function in the new one with a different culture is a complex process of change and adjustment. I made discoveries not only about my new country but about myself. Have I changed since I arrived here? I hope so. I also hope I have repaid this country which was, although tough, kind to and patient with me as I adjusted to the new life.

Soon after arrival, volunteers took us to different synagogues, organised holiday parties for us, and invited us to their homes. I still have a newspaper clip with Senator Graham's arm on my shoulder at a meeting at a synagogue. We had a special glorified place in American political culture and occupied a special spot in the immigrant pyramid. We were victims of Soviet repression and anti-Semitism saved by an altruistic America. They paraded us around as a living example of American superiority and a symbol of Soviet barbarism. We met

174

many interesting people and made connections. At one gathering, one of the volunteers offered to introduce me to the president of the congregation. *Maybe I can ask him to help me to find a job.*

"Mark," the president extended his arm.

"Yakov," I said. We shook hands.

"Any relationship to Yakov Smirnoff?" He grinned. *In America, is every Jacob related?*

"If you mean through vodka, the answer is yes."

"Oh, no, he is a famous Russian comedian," Mark said. I wasn't sure Mark got my quip. Here my sense of humour didn't work. Ironically, Smirnoff became a famous Russian by leaving Russia.

"At his concert," Mark continued, "he often said 'In America, you break the law. In Russia law breaks you.' You know his accent was heavier than yours, and he ignored the articles as my grandparents did. It added charm and authenticity to what he said. Oh wait, I remember another one, 'In America you assassinate presidents. In Russia presidents assassinate you.' Is it true?"

"Not literally, but yes." I didn't believe his accent was heavier than mine and thought Smirnoff exaggerated his accent and deliberately skipped the articles.

"How long has it been since you last been in a synagogue?" he asked next.

"Never," He stared at me with wide eyes and raised brows.

The expression on his face made it obvious that there was a need for explanation. Something more than 'never' seemed required. My limited English was too limited for an explanation, so I asked Anya for help.

"The synagogue in my shtetl was…" I glanced at Anya.

"What do you want to say?" she asked in Russian and took over. "It was confiscated by the state long before I was born. In Odessa, where I lived for the last thirty years, with a population of over one million people with a large Jewish presence, we had only one so-called synagogue that occupied a single room in an old building on the outskirts of the city."

"Have you been there?"

"I have never gone there for the fear of being watched by the KGB and reported to my place of employment." *When could I ask about employment?*

"Really?" Mark took a step back, his eyes wide.

"In our family, only my wife's grandfather went there to buy matzos for Passover. The two biggest synagogues in Odessa from before the revolution were a Party archive and a gym."

"Here in South Florida, we have dozens of synagogues," Mark said.

Now, I opened my eyes wide but immediately narrowed them and twisted my mouth, "Really?"

"Yes, really. So, now you can attend a synagogue whenever you want."

"How're you adjusting? Any problems?" He changed the conversation.

"I need a job."

"What did you do in Russia?"

"I was a teacher with a degree in physics."

I think he was impressed. He thought for a while, "You know, one of our congregants is the president of a local college. I will talk to him and call you."

"A week later, he called me with an appointment to meet the president at his school."

I was excited and fearful, and I called Anya.

"Your degree is called a Bachelor of Science here or B.S. for short," she said in English.

"Tell them you are willing to take any job." She switched back to Russian.

"How do I get there?"

After a moment of silence, she said, "I will arrange someone to pick you up."

I did everything she instructed me to do, but I didn't get a job. My lips quivered as I left his office. I thought, for the president, the meeting was just a formality. My degree was a B.S. in the other sense. A master's degree might help, a Ph.D. might be better. But for a Jew to get it, one had to be a genius.

Volunteers took us to synagogues often. Attending synagogues and participating in Jewish activities didn't make most of us religious. We were not religious people, far from that, but some things we did out of tradition and out of need. A far greater number of us sought to express our Jewishness through the celebration of Jewish social and cultural heritage. We still did what Jews were supposed to do. My daughter had a Jewish wedding with a Hoopa, glass breaking, and so on. My granddaughter had a Bat Mitzvah.

I was proud to hear her recite Hebrew prayers, even if both of us didn't understand a word. My grandson was circumcised and thirteen years later Bar Mitzvah in Jerusalem by the Wall.

My generation was a lost generation. My father had a Bar Mitzvah. He was born two decades before the Bolshevik revolution. My grandson had one. He was born in a free country. My opportunity was stolen by the brutal regime, as well as my choice to believe in God. I saw my grandsons Bar Mitzvah as a symbolic repudiation and reversal of Soviet attempts to deprive us of our heritage. My denial of the opportunity to embrace Jewish culture was repeated again and again across an entire generation—a lost Jewish generation. Now, I thought, my daughter's generation was too lost, but back in Russia, we even didn't hear about Bat Mitzvah.

Local Jews invited us for Shabbat dinners. They were interested in our stories and shared their families' stories with us. At one dinner, a guest asked for the vinaigrette. I was disappointed when instead of beet, potato, onion, and pickle salad the hostess brought a bottle of salad dressing. You inherit an arsenal of Russian traditions and superstitions that perplex Americans—like penchant for anything pickled—and simply don't translate into American culture. Pickled herring, topped with beets, onions, and mayonnaise don't make *selyodka pod shuboy* exciting for an American. Nor is kholodets attractive when described as 'meat jelly.' And for Americans vinaigrette is dressing not a salad.

I couldn't help thinking back to that last meal with my family and the salad that in Russia we called vinaigrette. Losing touch with the old country, with our language, with people we grew up with, through food, we tried to reconnect with our past. We still eat borscht for dinner, boiled potatoes with schmaltz herring for Sunday breakfast, and prefer vodka with it to other hard liquors. Memories aside, there was nothing to tie me to Russia but food and language.

Although we don't go to a synagogue often, we celebrate the Jewish New Year, we light menorahs on Hanukah, we bake or buy Hamantaschen on Purim, and have matzos for Passover.

After another dinner we were invited to, we all retired to the living room afterward. The host selected a tape from his collection and popped it into a VHS player. "You're going to love it. It's called Fiddler on the Roof." He looked at us.

"It's a musical that is based on Sholom Aleichem's novel," he explained when we didn't react.

"You do know Sholom Aleichem?"

"Yes, we do." I could finally give an affirmative answer.

"It's about a Jewish milkman and his daughters."

"Oh," I said. "It's called *Tevye the Milkman*." I pronounced the title in Yiddish.

We didn't take our eyes from the screen. When Tevye sang his famous aria *If I Were a Rich Man,* the memory of the toast I made at the last dinner using almost the same words made my eyes well.

Getting accustomed to new traditions, we wanted to keep the old ones. One of them was to get a New Year's tree. But we were told that was a Christian thing. In the communist Soviet Union, they had a New Year's tree even in Kremlin. The New Year was the most favourite holiday in the Soviet Union because it wasn't loaded with any political or ideological symbolism. It was full of wishes and hopes. It wasn't a religious thing, it was cultural.

"Why can't we have a tree?" Rika asked. She had a New Year tree every year since she was born.

"American Jews don't understand that it was our favourite holiday because it didn't have to do anything with communism."

"Apparently, all those New Year's family gatherings we had in the Soviet Union are meaningless to them," Mila said bitterly.

For our first New Year in America, we had a New Year tree anyway. We adorned with home-made decorations. Overwhelmingly, Soviet Jews, to put it bluntly, were not religious and didn't understand the meaning of the tree in

America. Although efforts had been made to integrate us, most remained apart from the Jewish community mainstream. But we still were Jews, proud Jews in a way how we understood Jewishness. Anyway, it was the last New Year's tree we had.

Like American Jews, our emigration is distinguished by a high level of skills and education. Unlike American Jews, we had minimum to zero exposure to the Jewish training and religion, and no experience with the organised Jewish community. Having spent more than seventy years living under the dictatorial and anti-religious regime, most Soviet Jews had only faded memories and tenuous ties to the Jewish religion. It's not our fault we became so detached from Jewish traditions back in the Soviet Union. In a few years, most of us transplants abandoned pretences to be religious and attended a synagogue only on Yom Kippur to honour our elders whose graves we left behind. But we celebrate the main Jewish holidays at family gatherings. We have a special dinner on Rosh Hashanah, a Seder for Passover, and light a menorah for Hanukah. My grandchildren liked Hanukah the most when they received Hanukah gelt (Yiddish for money). But it's cultural, not religious. One reason we fled to the States was in search of cultural freedom. We adopted irreligious, secular lives. We were grateful for our American brethren's persistent efforts to free us, but not in the ways they desired. We retained traces of Russian culture despite our genuine desire to assimilate. Although we share kinship ties with the many American Jews whose roots are also in the pre-communist Russian empire, our lives were shaped by different forces: the Bolshevik revolution, the suffering and losses of World War II, and the unique conditions of life in a communist state.

Chapter 32

A few weeks after our arrival, Alan took us to buy us sneakers. Our shoes didn't impress him. I thought he would take us to a shoe store. Instead, he brought us to a place called a mall. It was a gigantic space under a roof, air-conditioned. It even had trees inside. We passed a lot of stores with beautifully decorated windows, full of merchandise. Mila and Rika turned their heads from side to side, occasionally trying to stop for a better look. But Alan and Evelyn had a target destination in mind and led us towards it. A store we entered was full of nothing but shoes.

"Look at them all," my daughter said to Mila, "And in every colour of the rainbow." She picked up a pair of red high heels.

"May I help you," a saleswoman appeared from nowhere. But she didn't have a chance to help as Alan urged us to a part of the store where many dozens of sneakers were on display. Alan herded us to a wall of sneakers—Nike, Adidas, and other brands I never heard of.

"What size," Alan asked.

"Forty-one."

"Oh, no," he said. "Wait a minute." He looked around and a salesman materialized. "Do you know what European forty-one size is?"

"Yes, nine," the man said.

Even my footwear size is diminished.

"What are your sizes," I asked Mila and Rika.

"Thirty-eight and thirty-six," I said to Alan, pointing out to them.

He went to the shelves and, after looking for a while, brought me a pair of black Nike sneakers. Evelyn took care of the girls. I put the right one on and felt in heaven. I could barely manage to get on the left. For the women, it took a little longer. Mila and Rika had been more discriminate in their choices. Finally, we get to the cashier and Alan paid.

After shopping, they took us to lunch. We sat down in a clean café and Evelyn ordered something called a hamburger. The waitress brought five cutlets layered between the bread with something else inside. The aroma of freshly cooked meat filled the air and was enough to harden my arteries. The smell wafted up, travelled through my nostrils, and grabbed hold of my stomach. It made me drool and brought me back into my childhood. I had recalled the taste of my mother's—my favoured but rare—cutlets. It made me happy and sad at the same time. What we called cutlets, I learned later, Americans called patties. It looked appetizing and the smell was wonderful.

"What are you looking for?" Alan asked when he saw me looking around.

"Something to eat it with."

I said. "Oh, you just hold it with both hands, like this." He picked up his hamburger with two hands, pressing his fingers on the bun. "And you bite into it."

Can Americans open their mouths that wide? Maybe they can. When they smile their upper lips reveal the whole upper gum. My mouth doesn't open that wide.

After seeing Alan taking a bite, I picked my hamburger with care and tried a bite as he did.

"Be careful," Mila said in Russian.

My hamburger fell apart, spilling lettuce and dripping mayonnaise.

"I think I need a fork and a knife."

An immigrant who leaves the world that he had known his whole life is seldom prepared for what awaits him at his destination. The hamburger was a nuisance, not a problem. The journey from one world to a completely different one doesn't end when a new motherland welcomes its new child. It never ends. Helplessness smothers most newcomers, especially those who don't settle into an ethnic enclave, like Brighton Beach in New York. Things there were largely like they were in Odessa. It is even called a little Odessa. When instead you were plunged into mainstream America, life was more difficult, at least in the beginning. New York and other big cities had a dense concentration of low-level jobs coupled with public transportation, grocery stores, and pharmacies squeezed into a few blocks. There were many Russian speakers, which alleviated the crippling effect of the language barrier. Besides, Jewish organizations in those cities had more than a century of experience welcoming and helping emigrants. The experiences of Soviet Jews arriving into big cities, like New York, had been quite distinctive from ours as we were one of the first Soviet Jews in the area. The entire Russian enclave in Broward County consisted of us, two other recently arrived families, and a few old-timers who arrived in America a decade earlier and later moved to the greater Miami area. One of the old-timers was Anya whom the Jewish federation hired to work with us. They understood that the best person to relate to a new immigrant was the one that had already assimilated. She was a nice person and did her best to help us. Unfortunately, she had no experience working with immigrants.

She helped us to open a checking account and taught us how to write a check. She explained other things that people in America take in with Mother's milk. She recommended an affordable rental for $500. The next day, we went to see the place. Anya came to Alan's development, and he followed her with all of us in his car. When we arrived, Anya told us it is a townhouse and explained what it means.

"Go and look at it," Anya said when we were inside. Mila went to the kitchen and Rika to the living room.

"Where are the other rooms?" I asked.

"Upstairs," Anya pointed to the stairs.

Wow. I hurried up. There were two bedrooms and two bathrooms there.

"What do you think?" I asked Mila.

"It's beautiful." It smelled of new paint and carpet.

I looked at Rika. "It has three bathrooms," she said giggling.

"We will take it," I said to Alan nodding quickly. "It's more than we dreamed of."

"No, you're not," Allan shook his head.

"Why not?"

"Not now," he said. "I'll explain it later." Then he turned to Anya. "You suppose to know better."

She didn't say anything.

"Alan, why you didn't like the area?" I said at home, Mila and Rika listened.

"Did you see the cars over there?"

"Yes, there was a car almost at all houses."

"In Russia, almost no one had a car," Rika said.

"The cars were inexpensive and old. It's a poor area. It's not safe here." After a pause, Alan said, "We would worry about the house when you find a job."

"How do I look for a job?" I bombarded Alan with questions. Some amused him, some annoyed, and some did both at the same time.

"Look in the newspaper," he said. "That's where they advertise jobs."

Two newspapers I was most familiar with were *Pravda (Truth)* and *Izvestia (News)*. I never saw job advertisements in those or any other newspapers. I never saw any advertisements in Soviet newspapers. They were filled with news, real or concocted—good news anywhere east of East Germany, and bad news anywhere west of West Germany. As a joke went, *there is no news in Pravda (Truth) and no truth in Izvestia (News)*. A job advertisement in those? Come to think about this. Alan showed me the Classifieds section of the *Sun Sentinel* and explained what it is.

"I'm so grateful to you for answering my questions. I can't find words to express it."

"No applause." He smiled. "Just throw money." It took me a while to figure out it was a joke.

"What?" I said.

"It's a Vaudeville."

"What's a vaudeville?"

"Ahh Yakov, you have a lot to learn about America, Vaudeville is a style of entertainment and jokes from the 1920s." I nodded, pretending to understand.

Chapter 33

The next morning, once the newspaper arrived, we picked a few candidates and after breakfast went job hunting with high hopes. But reality set in as days became weeks. A few ads and, after breakfast, went to check them. We were not successful. We did the same thing for a while, and the interviewers all said the same thing, "It's a recession. Jobs are scarce." Recession and scarce were some of the first English words I learned in America. The following days were ones of the most frustrating in my American life. Nobody was hiring, and Alan was getting tired of being a chauffeur.

My ambition to find a decent job, after a couple of weeks, was pretty much squelched, and I was ready to work in any capacity—anything, just to work. Of all my goals only one had endured—survival. I never dreamed it would be hard to find work in America. I thought in such a rich country everyone could find work to support a family. I still don't fully understand why it's not so.

After many unsuccessful attempts to find a job, Evelyn said that Alan grew tired of driving us around, and I was frustrated and desperate. Finally, my luck turned. A chain of craft stores that were opening a few stores in the region hired everyone who applied. I was assigned to a store in Coral Springs. Things were looking up. Only I couldn't afford a car. A few days Alan drove me to the store, but the solution was to find an apartment within a walking distance from the store. We were lucky to find a rental for $500 a month with a fifteen minutes' walk to the store. Coral Springs was nicer than Margate where Alan lived.

"You just came to the country and will be living where rich people live." He smiled. "And you will be earning $5.50 an hour. A t my first job I'd got only $0.50."

"And how much did you pay for rent?"

"Yeah, you are right." He closed his eyes.

It was a two-bedroom, one-bathroom apartment, not as nice as the townhouse we saw, but still better than what we had in the old country.

They assigned me to the framing department and told me they will train me how to frame pictures. In the first couple of weeks, we worked on preparing the store for the grand opening: cleaning, installing shelves and equipment, and decorating. Because of my language problem, I did mostly the cleaning. Even such a simple job required basic language. One day I was asked to find a mop. So, I went and asked a man for a map. "Why do you need a map," he asked me. It took a few moments until I clarified what I need by pantomiming a sweeping motion. The company wanted to open its stores as soon as possible, so it was a lot of overtime. It fitted me well. But just my salary wasn't enough to keep the roof over our heads. Mila would need to work too. I asked the manager of my store if he had a job for my wife. He explained that the company's policy was not to allow relatives to work at the same store, but he could refer her to one of the other stores opening in the region.

"Mila, I found a job for you." I came home elated. At last, I felt in control.

"Where?" She smiled.

"At another store like mine." My words erased the smile faster than I used to erase a word from a chalkboard.

"But I don't have a car."

"You are lucky. I have already checked and you can reach it with no trouble by bus."

Immigration is never easy. Whether with self-esteem, social status, or health, one way or another, every immigrant pays his dues, the price of admission to America. Sweat, blood, and patience were entry charges for the opportunity to pursue happiness and achieve the proverbial American dream. The older you are, the steeper the fare. But with two salaries, our lives improved'

Now, we had to learn a lot—first, how to shop for groceries. Thankfully, The Publix supermarket was a few blocks away from where we lived. We came to America at the beginning of September, and now, in mid-October, when we went shopping by ourselves for the first time, the supermarket was still a miracle; really *super*—the size, the colours, and the abundance of food. Smiling cashiers, who said hello and asked how I am doing, made me wonder what made me so special. In Soviet stores, everything was more understandable. Back home, salespeople frowned, and customers recoiled. Rudeness was ordinary and familiar in the Soviet Union, a way of life adopted by people deprived of the most basic things. Cashiers couldn't afford and were not required to smile at customers. People with authority, no matter how small, had the upper hand and the rest of us complied. The supermarket looked to me as if my partial colour-blindness was miraculously and at once cured. Mila and Rika were carried away with the shopping cart, mesmerized by the display of dozens of kinds of cheeses, frozen pizzas, and multi-coloured produce department. Prices brought them to the real world fast, and they slowed down to find the least expensive deals. You were lost in a supermarket if you couldn't read the labels. Even if you can read, you are lost if you don't understand what you are reading. In a while, when I could read and understand the labels, I didn't understand why one needs ten brands of toothpaste. With just one, I wouldn't need to spend ten minutes to pick. The whole process of making choices and becoming a consumer was difficult. It was easier to shop in Odessa where queues always led to products available at the moment, eliminating the necessity of making choices. In Odessa, I made it a habit to first join any queue before asking what it was for.

We didn't have a car yet and had to walk to the supermarket. Thankfully, it was only a few blocks from our apartment. When the three of us walked back with a bag in each hand, the cars sometimes honked at us. I didn't understand why. Later, I figured out it was entertaining for people.

In the beginning, we were lonely. Having no friends but one, any extended family, and little ability to communicate made us holed up in our apartment. If you don't have a car, you can't get around in South Florida. Despite the confusion, we were happy, especially because for a few weeks there was a lot of overtime preparing the stores for the grand opening, and we desperately needed money. In a few weeks, they started cutting the overtime, and in a while began laying people off. I didn't understand what's happening. They opened the stores during the recession, a co-worker explained to me. One day Mila came home and I, looking at her face said, "What's wrong?"

"I lost my job," she said. She averted her eyes.

"It's not your fault. They fire a lot of people. We will find something else."

"Yeah. What about your job?" Her voice cracked.

That's when a powerful factor entered our lives—fear. It wasn't fear of the State like in the old country. This was a different fear—of not finding a job, of not having money to pay rent, of not having a place to live. Because there was no stability, that fear of hanging over a precipice stayed with us until I was laid off right before Christmas. The fear multiplied. Life in a Socialist system didn't prepare us for such circumstances. Infantilism was characteristic of Soviet people because we were never responsible for much. We had a secure job and a place to live—both all but for life. When you are thrown into the water and don't know how to swim, the survival instincts are what drive you. But sometimes, with some people, they don't work and you go under. Unfortunately, because of my psychological makeup, I was one such person. During the weeks that followed, I experienced alternative waves of despair and anger—with passing days, less angry, and more desperate. Then, when you thought it couldn't get any worse, the despair ultimately wins. I was defeated. Worse than the defeat itself, perhaps, is feeling helpless in defeat. A person can survive anything as long as he sees the end in sight. I didn't. Depression is so insidious that it makes it impossible to see the end. Depression, anxiety, and high blood pressure were common occurrences at least during the first year. Of course, not all émigrés responded the same way.

The 1990s started with me and Mila unemployed, the economy still in recession, and me in depression. I soon learned that living in America is more stressful than in Russia. I was wracked with self-doubt but knew that going back is not an option. I felt trapped. A sudden and dramatic loss of income and status had taken a profound psychological and emotional toll on me because I was denied my place as protector and primary provider. I tried to keep my mind positive, but the mind goes wherever it wants. When you are depressed, you don't control your thoughts, your thoughts control you. That happened to me. It was the end. Without a job, the future looked bleak. I didn't see the way out of my situation. I wanted to sleep and escape from hell, at least for a while. But sleep wouldn't come. I lay in bed and terrible thoughts played in my head like on a loop. Every minute felt like an hour and every hour like an eternity. In the morning, I didn't want to get up, I wanted to fall asleep again and never wake up. Conscious thoughts about my family couldn't penetrate the wall of despair. I didn't want to live, but I didn't have the energy to do anything about that.

People think depression is sadness. But people are wrong. Depression is darkness 24/7, it's beyond sadness. It's being a black-and-white person in a multi-coloured world. It's hell inside your mind. Everything is an effort, from something as big as facing people to as small as moving. I spent a lot of energy to prevent people from realising how I felt. My lips said "Fine, thanks," but my eyes told a different story. People didn't pay attention, so I could fool them. But I couldn't fool Mila.

"What's going on?" she asked me.

"I don't know."

I didn't know. I had no idea what depression was. In the Soviet Union, people usually didn't know about depression. They thought it's just sadness and if you can't overcome it, you lack willpower. It is difficult to describe depression to one who hasn't experienced the insanity of it. Imagine my situation, no language to express my feelings—I doubt I could express them in my native language—and no health insurance. Now, I understood Alan's words about health insurance.

Every immigrant expected something from America; otherwise, why go through the torturous process. In the end, it paid off, but in the beginning, you didn't know that it would. I came to the frightening realisation that all my knowledge and experience were now virtually useless, and this is not a vacation, this is forever. I never imagined that the 'crap' people talked about we have to eat until it becomes better would be so bad. Facing the unexpected can quickly derail your plans and trim down your optimism. I responded by being severely depressed. There is a complacency that comes with helplessness, a strange relief in giving up. Depression drained me of any remaining energy and prevented me from taking action to improve the situation. I felt evicted from life. The Jewish Federation again helped. They found a job for me at a synagogue. It didn't help morally, but it helped materially. The job afforded me time to figure out what to do.

Yet, amid my misery, new optimism and determination bit by bit awoke. I started to undertake tentative steps to solve the situation.

"Rabbi," I asked the rabbi for advice. "I can't be a teacher now. I don't have any other skills. What would you advise me?"

"You know, they say that the easier license to obtain is a real estate license. Maybe you should try this." He smiled and added, "Although the rumour is there are more real estate licenses in Florida than driver licenses." Only when I became a realtor, I understood why he was smiling.

I enrolled in a real estate school the next day. With the help of the dictionary, I went through the school and passed the exam near the top of the class. The next step was the State exam. Without a delay, I made an appointment and in a few weeks, was driving to Miami for the exam. It was a long drive. I listened to the radio. My favourite station was NPR. Besides learning something, it helped me with the language. When they announced the coup in Moscow against Gorbachev, my heart sank. During the exam, I forced myself not to think about the coup. After the exam, I worried not only if I passed but about what's going on in the Soviet Union meant for the relatives left there. When I came home, I rushed inside.

"Did you pass?" Mila grinned.

"We will find out. Did you watch TV?" She shook her head. "There is a coup in Moscow, they imposed a state of emergency."

"The state of emergency, what does it mean?" She leaned forward.

"It means that Gorbachev is out, and they will turn the clock back." I bit my lip.

"I would never see my family again? Would they be trapped forever behind the new Iron Curtain?"

"Let's hope not. Meanwhile, let's start the process of bringing the family to the United States even if they didn't ask yet."

Life had already taught me that nothing is permanent but death. After the unsuccessful coup, on December 26, 1991, the Soviet Union died, after a long and painful decline, a peaceful, as it looked at the time, death. It was 74 years old. The words 'unbroken union of free republics united forever by mighty Russia' from the Soviet Anthem I memorized in first grade came to mind. How pathetic the words 'unbroken, free, and forever' sounded after the Soviet Union's demise. After that, it didn't take long for the family to ask. We were prepared.

With the collapse, the Soviet Union lost the Cold War. In my opinion, American politicians misunderstood the Soviet loss for American win. Instead of a more limited and achievable foreign policy, policymakers believed that the United States, at a minimal cost and risk, could act on its imperatives. The 1990s were a lost opportunity for international cooperation when the seeds of new animosity and a new Cold War were planted. American politicians believed that the country could only be safe if the world looked more like the country and abided by the will of the United States. Gradually, throughout a generation, the United States has become less and less able to afford global predominance.

For a few weeks, I checked the mailbox every day, before I received my real estate license. Getting the license was the easier part of becoming a realtor. Starting making money was not so easy.

"What I have to do to make money?" I asked my broker.

"You have to prospect."

"You," he reacted to my blank stare, "must let people know you are a realtor, make calls, and walk the streets." After a pause, he added, "That will be enough to start."

Letting people know I am a realtor was relatively easy. Most people I knew spoke Russian. Making calls and speaking to people on the streets I needed English.

Chapter 34

Learning English was the second problem. Even if you understand the basics, people still struggle to understand you with your accent, improper grammar, and incorrect usage of certain words. They now and then made remarks that upset me.

"Are you Russian mafia?" they asked.

"No, I KGB," I began to answer when I got tired of it, deliberately omitting the 'am' as we did in Russian. When they asked me if I am KGB, I answered, "No, I mafia."

Learning the language is deeper than just vocabulary, even than grammar. There is another dimension to it—it's about understanding the culture, the body language, and the psychology of people who grew up in this country. The other English language, made up not just of words but also facial expressions and habits of conversations, is even harder to master. And idioms. Oy vey! This takes time, and the best you can do is practice while exposing yourself to American culture. You are expected to learn English, except you're working a menial job where your exposure to the language is minimal. I had trouble with grammatical rules; and all the words, so many new words to learn. I wrote down words on cards and kept them in my pockets. Whenever I had a chance, I looked up the words. Some words stuck, others didn't. Sometimes I remembered the card number the word was on and the exact location of the word, but not the meaning. It was a torturous process to expand my vocabulary. You have to make an effort to learn the language: attend free classes, find opportunities to talk to locals, and reading. I did all of these as much as I could. But the progress was slow.

I asked a volunteer, who sometimes checked on our progress, "What can I do to learn the language faster."

"Talk to people and listen."

"Where?"

"Where? Find groups where you can practice your English. Uhm… look them up in the local newspaper."

I bought the local newspaper the next day and found the relevant information in the local section. I still remember the name Kiwanis that told me nothing. So were the rest but one that caught my eyes and imagination—Toastmasters, because toast and master are also Russian words with the same meaning. So, this made the most sense for me. I pictured people gathering around a table, filling glasses with vodka, and mastering the art of toasting. I immediately called to find out where and when is the next meeting. I was a little surprised that it was at a school but still hopeful and enthusiastic.

Next Wednesday, I was at the school with a bottle of vodka in a bag. When I found the room, instead of a big table there were student's desks with adults behind them. I tried to hide the bag when a woman I talked to on the phone, approached me. After a short conversation, she pointed to a desk, and I sat.

The meeting started with introductions. Every person stood up, pointed a hand towards the toastmaster of the meeting, and said, "Madam Toastmaster, I am *First Name and Last Name*." Then with the same gesture towards her, "Madam Toastmaster." When the last person introduced himself, the toastmaster asked me if I would like to introduce myself. I stood up awkwardly. I couldn't force myself to raise my hand. The word madam I met only in books describing the pre-Revolutionary life. It was a bourgeois word. During the whole Soviet period, we had problems addressing people whose names we didn't know because words equivalent to 'mister' and 'misses' were also considered bourgeois. We awkwardly called them 'man' and 'woman'. I just said, "I am Yakov Grinshpun."

Next, a person called "word-master," introduced a new word. He explained the meaning of the word, gave examples of its usage, and urged us to use it during the meeting. I still remember the word I had learned at the first meeting— *plethora,* and I remembered its meaning. I had a plethora to learn about America. Learning a new word compensated, in part, for the disappointment that no real toast would be given.

Next were impromptu speeches.

"Now, we will be talking of the cuff," the toastmaster addressed me. I nodded as if I understood. At home, I looked up the word calf and still couldn't make sense of what he meant.

The rest of the session was a series of prepared speeches by the members. Each speaker had an assigned evaluator.

"Evaluators were encouraged to use the Oreo cookie model of evaluation," the toastmaster explained for my benefit. "Like the cookie, the evaluation consists of three parts. Start with a compliment, suggest improvements, and finish with encouragement."

It was a new concept to me. We, in the Soviet Union, were trained to criticize when evaluating. That's what we did after attending the 'open lessons' of fellow teachers. It's still easier for me to criticize than to praise.

In the beginning, I understood about a quarter of what was said, but it was an immersion into English. So, I stuck with the group. Each week I learned at least one new word, and little by little the language became more comfortable. With each meeting, I understood more of what was being said. One day, I decided that I was ready to give a short speech. And I did. No small feat. It didn't matter that people understood maybe a quarter of what I said. What mattered was that I stood up and spoke. In English! With time people understood me more and I felt more relaxed when giving speeches and more confident; so, confident that I brought humour into my speeches.

One day, Caren Neale, who was the emcee for the regional competition of Toastmasters clubs, asked me if I can entertain people with humour before the competition starts. Caren spoke so well that I listened to her speeches like to a beautiful song. Besides, she never refused to help. She even suggested for me to start writing in English. When I started to write, she invited me to her group of fellow writers. If not for her, I doubt I would dare to write.

It was hard to say yes. By nature, I am rather shy than bold. What I mean is that I do afraid of doing uncomfortable things, but I am courageous. Despite the fear, I do what I need to do. Besides, I couldn't say no to Caren. So, I did say yes. To this day I am grateful to Caren because this event transformed me. Now I had to prove her confidence in me. I had prepared a few jokes and, before the event, tested them on my family and friends.

"Once, a priest and a rabbi…"

"No, no," Mila interrupted me. "You would offend religious people."

"A democrat and a republican sat in a bar…"

"That's a big no," Emma cut me short. "Never talk politics to people you don't know well."

Burdened with the fear of failing Caren, I became obsessed with finding a topic that would offend no one. Finally, I found a topic that would upset no one. I had prepared a few good jokes and was ready to confront my fears.

"Are you ready?" Caren asked when I arrived at the competition.

"Yes."

I came back with an enthusiastic, "And what will you be talking about?"

"Sex!"

"NO! We don't do that at Toastmasters."

You don't do it? I'm quitting.

Toastmasters taught me to pay attention to somebody's words before responding. So before quitting, I clarified what she meant.

"What do you mean you don't do *that*?"

"We don't talk about sex at Toastmasters."

Doing and talking are different things. I'm not quitting yet.

A few minutes and nothing to talk about.

I stepped up before the group. I told the whole story of how I have prepared for this event and what happened a few minutes earlier. "Here I am before you without a thing to talk about." People were sympathetic, and they laughed. I think they found the story funny. Toastmasters taught me to think on my feet. I told a few political jokes that could offend nobody because they were about Soviet politics. I remember one that was received well.

-An American and a Russian arguing about their two countries. And the American says, "Look, can walk in the Oval Office, pound the desk and say, 'Mr President, I don't like the way you are running the country.'"

The Russian says, "I can do that."

"You can?"

"I can go to the Kremlin pound his desk and say, 'Comrade General Secretary, I don't like how President Reagan is running his country'."

I was with the Toastmasters for a decade. They helped me tremendously. My English proficiency increased and that allowed me not only for new opportunities but also to establish better relationships and interactions with local people. Toastmaster didn't solve all my language problems. You can learn to speak a language, but until you know and understand the culture you will never really be fluent in that language.

Besides the lower income, lack of adequate language skills incurred psychological damage. One of my feelings of loss had been that I no longer could assist my daughter. In the Soviet Union, there was a joke, "What kind of a parent you are if you can't support your children until they retire." I also wasn't able to call in favours for her; all my life-long connections were useless. All I could do was hope that she will do it on her own.

Fortunately, in this country, my daughter was able to achieve on her own. She thinks so also. Sometimes, I remind her that we have a part in it too—either through genes, her upbringing, or, rather, both. We had come to America with a few hundred dollars for the three of us and no tangible assets. Yet, we had intangible assets: education, willingness to take risks and to work hard, and determination. And we had each other. Despite all the difficulties, abandoning everything you have and know and moving half a world away in search of freedom and opportunities was the smartest decision I have ever made, besides marrying my wife.

In December 1992, Rika got married. Unlike us, she was married not by local authorities, but, in the Jewish tradition, under a hupa with a rabbi officiating the vows. She found her happiness with a nice Russian Jewish man, Alex. He is a good husband and the best son-in-law we could dream of. I wish I could erase the in-law part. They didn't waste time, and a year later, my granddaughter, Sabina was born. A few years later, my grandson, Michael was born. Having grandchildren is to love them like your own children, only to lavish much more attention that I failed to give my own daughter. Without a question, one of the most meaningful achievements of my life is that my grandchildren were born in a free country with all possibilities open to them. Unlike me, they never experienced discrimination and shortages—be it of opportunities, food, or freedom.

Chapter 35

In 1993 Mila's parents and her sister with her family arrived. They were as unprepared as we were, but at least they had a family to help. We rented and furnished an apartment for the sister's family and took the parents to live with us. For a few months, I was busy driving them around to different appointments. I had hardly had time to do anything else. As a realtor, I had flexibility with my time. They say that time is money, so I paid for the time with the money that I didn't earn. Sasha, my son-in-law, helped my brother-in-law Valeriy to find a job. Although immigration is difficult for everyone, it was a little easier for them than it was for us. We had three years of immigration experience ready to help them.

As for the parents, who were over 65, as refugees, they were eligible for Medicare, Medicaid, SSI, and housing assistance. They spoke Yiddish that helped them to communicate with a large population of elderly Jews in South Florida. It seemed to me it was easier for people over 65. Now, when I reached their age, I understand it was difficult for them as well. They were highly professional. My mother-in-law was a pharmacist, and my father-in-law was an artist. My daughter's in-laws were both doctors. Elderly people were like plants that had been taken from one soil to another. They withered and weakened, not only physically, and combated their misery in many ways, including shopping trips to supermarkets. They needed time to make new roots. My mother-in-law collected coupons and looked-for sales. When I would bring both of them to a supermarket, where they spent more than an hour, it was for them as a trip to a theatre, especially when they discussed how much money they saved. They didn't hold on to every kopek as most people did back in the Soviet Union, but when kopeks became cents in America, my mother-in-law would hold on to them like a lifeline. Although time was money for me, I understood how important it was for them. Trips to doctors were my responsibility also because, in South Florida, there was almost no public transportation. It was difficult to find doctors that accept Medicaid. Usually, it was far from where they lived. Besides, I served as their interpreter. It wasn't always comfortable for them to discuss their medical problems with me being there.

In many, the conflict between accepting and even valuing dependence and striving for freedom had created strong feelings of guilt and humiliation. Some people expressed it as shame at having been duped by Soviet ideology, others felt ashamed at having been made victims, unable to help their families. Many found relief in talking with friends and relatives on the phone. Unlike in the old country, everyone had a phone. They discussed the news from local Russian language newspapers, the coupons from English language newspapers, and TV shows, like Wheel of Fortune, that didn't require mastery of English. Immigration is never easy. It is often a process that strips people of dignity, in ways big and small.

Most Soviet Jews applied to become citizens as soon as they were eligible. We became eligible for naturalization in 1995, six years after we came to America. For more than six years we lived statelessly. For the swearing-in, we drove to Miami from Boca Raton, citizens of no country. We drove back with certificates in our hands, citizens of a great country. This evening, we celebrated the event with our relatives and friends. After we became citizens, we applied for passports. We held our passports and looked at each other. I opened mine. "There is no fifth line." My U.S. passport—unlike my former Soviet one—didn't list my ethnicity. I was an American like everyone else, but I didn't feel like one yet. Although the American part of my Russian-American identity was growing larger and larger, the shrinking Russian part was still noticeably present. We immediately registered to vote. We registered as Democrats. In 1996, I was able to participate in my first free elections. For the first time in my life, I felt that my vote matters. And it did. The candidate I had voted for won. When he left the office, I voted for another candidate and felt that my vote didn't matter. It was the 2000 elections.

We were Americans, and we were happy. For more than two decades in the country, we lived as normal a life as was possible under the circumstances. Life was as good as we could have hoped for until the disaster struck. Mila was diagnosed with cancer in the fall of 2013. It is stunning how little time it takes to go from trouble to tragedy.

In the spring of next year, Mila passed away. She had gone. I would never see her again, alone on a loveseat built for two, with a void in my chest, as though something had fallen out of me. Where love goes when one dies? There was also a void in my bed. I couldn't sleep at night; my bed was too wide. When I woke up in the middle of the night and habitually put my hand to the other side of the bed, it was cold. Lying in my dump sheets, I listened to my heart. Her face stared out of the picture on the nightstand. It seemed already to be yellowing. I closed my eyes. *This couldn't be happening to me, to us.* But even though I closed my eyes, the picture continued to go around in my head. *How would I go to live without her?* I never expected to be a widower. She was younger and healthier. All I wanted to is to scream. All I did, in the end, was quietly sobbed.

The first month after she died, I would burst into tears when reflecting on Mila's death or the future we would not share. I couldn't believe I wouldn't see her eyes or hear her laugh again. I thought I'd never learned to live without her. Bereft and brimming with grief, I was angry at the whole world: doctors who missed and intervened when it was too late, old couples holding hands, old ladies who were barely moving. Why Mila when others live well into their ninetieth? Grief wore me down. There was a mountain of grief to be climbed. And no talk, like you have to be strong, you have to live your life, just cherish your memories wouldn't help until I reached the summit and began the long and difficult descent. Besides grief, another feeling was guilt. Why *I* missed it? Have I done everything to save her?

The descend began one day when I resumed substitute teaching. I sat in the teacher's planning room, staring at nothing, and felt tears building up in the corners of my eyes.

"How you've been, I didn't see for a long time." A fellow substitute teacher with whom I became friends said.

"My wife passed away." I started to well up. He put his hand on my shoulder. I held my tears back.

After a long moment, he said, "I'm sorry. I understand how you feel." I just stared at him. "I do understand, I lost my wife twenty years ago."

"So, you are alone."

"No, I remarried."

"How did you ever get over it?"

"You don't ever get over the pain." After a pause, "You just learn to live with it."

I was a slow learner. It took me four and a half years to learn. Learning to live without her, I knew my love would live with me forever, a dull ache that would never go away. I realised, after what I lived through, that life is so fragile. For the most part, I tried to block the thoughts of how easily life could be torn asunder. Most of the time, these thoughts were hidden deep down. But when they surfaced from the depth of the subconscious, I understood how thin the line is. At these moments, it was not that I couldn't accept the truth about life's fragility, it was that I couldn't block the thoughts. One of the strange things about grief was when I thought I had enough grief to last a lifetime, it ambushed me when I least expected it.

My daughter and her family, my job, my writing, and, of course, my memories are what make my life worth living.

Epilogue
I Am an American

When asked what I am, I no longer hesitate—Am I Jewish? Am I Russian? Am I Russian-American?—I settled, when people asked me who I am, on "I am an American." Not Russian, not Russian-American, just American. It took me many years after becoming a legal citizen to realise that I am a real American.

I began to feel American when I stopped thinking about Americans as *them* but as *us* and ceased considering English a foreign language. I *am* an American because I understand what it means and possibly appreciate it more than many who were born here. Sometimes, having a perspective from afar brings life into better focus.

Being an American means I can make my own decisions free to reject what the government, media, and anyone else tell me about what and who I am. Here, I have learned that I am free to reject what the government, media, or other people try to tell me about whom and what I am.

Being an American means I am not afraid to speak my mind, and I can live wherever I can afford instead of a random stamp in my Soviet internal passport choosing for me.

Being an American means my daughter and my grandchildren and I can apply to any college or for any job without the fear of discrimination. Here there is no fifth lane in any document as it was in my Soviet passport stating 'Jew'.

Being an American is an honour and a privilege.

Most of all, America is a free country. But nothing is free here. For everything I wanted, I had to work hard. The greatness of this country is that it rewards hard work. America gave me and my family the tools to succeed—opportunities, freedom of choice, and incentive to do our best.

America accepted me, and I accepted America. Until you accept this country with all its imperfections, until you feel that it's your country, this country won't accept you. The United States is like a mirror.

I came to this country at the age of 46 with rudimentary English and basically without a profession because without the language there was no way to be a teacher. I had no other skills. To survive I had to do what in my worst dreams I didn't imagine I would be doing. We had to start from scratch but we survived. Over years of despair, depression, and hopelessness, I learned the language and received a real estate license. I didn't become rich, but I made a comfortable living. Mastering the language led me to participate in social life outside the Russian-speaking community. Now I am a member of a few meet-up groups and a published author. In English, no less.

My wife, with no English at all, did whatever she could to support the family. She learned the language by watching TV and reading Agatha Christie's novels. I think she had read all of her books. When she started to understand a little and form simple sentences, she obtained nail and facial licenses and earned an income. Eventually, she began working for herself.

We achieved the American dream.

Like many parents, the main reason we undertook this difficult endeavour was the future of our daughter. Is my daughter happy that we brought her here? Yes, unequivocally! She had educational opportunities not available for her in the Soviet Union. Math and engineering were the only ones available to Soviet Jews. She obtained a degree in mathematics just before we left the Soviet Union. While working as a cashier in her first year here, she improved her English and was accepted to Florida Atlantic University to study programming with all credits accepted and transferred from Odessa State University. It wasn't her first choice, but she couldn't afford to spend four years to obtain a different degree because money was an issue. After being a Florida resident for a year, in-state tuition was affordable for us. We helped her to start, and she took off. She was never refused a job because she was Jewish. Her Jewish heritage never came up. After about twenty years as a computer programmer, she decided to pursue her dream not available to her as a Jew in the Soviet Union. She became a pharmacist. In Russia, she was barred from pharmacy school before she was conceived. She made me proud, achieving something impossible in the old country. These were the choices and opportunities we were offered. Hard work paid off.

As for my grandchildren, who were born here, they are Americans through and through. They are the proof I made the right decision and did for them what I wish my grandparents did for me. Sabina graduated from the University of Florida and received a master's degree from NYU. She has been accepted to a medical school to chase her dream. Michael graduated from Florida State University. They don't know what the fifth line is.

We are grateful Americans for the opportunity to pursue happiness. And I am also grateful to this country for the opportunity to call myself an American while simultaneously calling myself a Jew. In the old country, I didn't have this luxury. I was a Jew and never could call myself a Russian. The most they allowed is to call myself a Russian Jew. Here, I am a proud American and a proud Jew. I am a Jewish American.

When I decided that I am done with Russia, life unpleasantly reminded me that maybe I'm not. To be a first-generation Russian-American is rather a nutty experience. I thought my Russian past was just that, the past. It was wishful thinking. As a 'Russian', the identity I was born with, I am now associated less with Tolstoy and Dostoevsky, and more with election interference. Yet, as an American, my hard-earned new identity, I am a citizen of the very democracy that Russians are blamed to have sabotaged. Not since McCarthy has Russia been so present in the American mind. But being present is not the same as being known. How the media presents Russia suffers from exaggeration, paranoia, and clichés. For about five years, I watched America's political elite and media shift the blame for our domestic political problems away from the United States and onto invented foreign enemies—Russia is number one among them. Yes, the countries are different, but it doesn't mean they have to be enemies.

One meeting allowed me to see the matter from a different perspective. In the fall of 2018, I attended a Russian picnic in a park. In Florida, the arrival of fall brings slightly cooler temperatures. The weather is quite agreeable to spending time outdoors. The tables in the part of the park designated as a picnic area were generously served with home-made Russian food. There were latkes, gefilte fish, pickles, vinaigrette. Coolers were stuffed with soda, beer, and, of course, vodka. The memory brought me back to the last dinner in the Soviet Union. People cling to their culinary memories.

I remember this picnic not because of the food but because of the man I had met there and the conversation I had with him. He was born in America to a famous noble family which escaped Russia after the Bolshevik revolution. It was a time of the intense anti-Russian campaign in America after the 2016 elections, so I was interested in his opinion of the relationships between the two countries.

"What do you think about the new cold war that it seems started between new Russia and America?" I asked. "The countries are so different, but it doesn't mean they have to be at war."

"They are not so different." He said. "In fact, they have a lot in common."

At this moment, I remembered me contrasting the countries on a flight from Moscow about thirty years ago.

"By the way," he added. "If you are looking for differences, you can find plenty of them. But if you looking for similarities, you can find plenty of them also."

"Can you compare them for me?"

"I can compare them for the whole day." He smiled. "I know the histories of both very well."

"I'm listening." I was sceptical.

"Both countries are huge multi-ethnic melting pots that are federal republics, and both have flags with blue, white, and red as their colours."

I couldn't argue with this, so I just said, "Uh-huh. But it doesn't make them friends."

"Both had one foot in Europe, with its old-world refinement, and the other in their vast rural hinterlands they conquered from the natives." He looked at me as if considering if it makes sense to continue. After a delay, he said, "Their largest demographic groups are Caucasian and their largest religious denominations are Christian."

"Okay, that could potentially make them friends," I agreed.

"They both had the temerity to implement radical regime-threatening political philosophies long-discussed theoretically in Europe—American Revolution and the Communist Revolution. And both are not averse to messianic ideas and belief in their unique paths."

He is well educated and read, I thought.

"You want more?" I nodded. "Both countries became superpowers as a result of winning World War II."

At least, I still am a citizen of a superpower.

"And both are still weapon and space superpowers," he said as if reading my thoughts.

"They have more in common," he said extending his hand. "Just think about it—Alaska and Afghanistan for example."

Before departing, he added, "Unfortunately, the Russian revolution wasn't good for the country."

When he moved away, I thought that America is much more like Russia than I cared to admit.

Afterward, I assumed that maybe they could become allies, if not friends, in the future in the war of civilizations some were talking about. Thirty years had passed since I came to America, and yet my Russian past still had a grip on me. I think Russia is buried in my head like my reptilian brain.

Am I glad that I escaped from form Russia? Absolutely. Do I hate Russia? No. Do I like Russia? Neither. Do I care about Russia? A little. Russia is a part of me and I wish her well.

Do I like America? No. I love America with all its imperfections. America isn't perfect, but it still awes me. I came to America hoping to improve life for my family, and the country gave me the opportunity. For that, I am grateful forever.

From Russia with hope, in America to stay to live the life I love.